THICKER THAN
BLOOD

THICKER THAN
BLOOD
ADOPTIVE PARENTING
IN THE MODERN WORLD

MARION CROOK

ARSENAL PULP PRESS
VANCOUVER

ARSENAL PULP PRESS
Suite 202 – 211 East Georgia St.
Vancouver, BC V6A 1Z6
Canada
arsenalpulp.com

The publisher gratefully acknowledges the support of the Canada Council for the Arts and the British Columbia Arts Council for its publishing program, and the Government of Canada (through the Canada Book Fund) and the Government of British Columbia (through the Book Publishing Tax Credit Program) for its publishing activities.

Cover and text design and cover illustration by Oliver McPartlin
Printed and bound in Canada

Library and Archives Canada Cataloguing in Publication
 Crook, Marion, 1941-, author
    Thicker than blood : adoptive parenting in the modern
world / Marion Crook.

Includes bibliographical references and index.
Issued in print and electronic formats.
ISBN 978-1-55152-631-7 (paperback).—ISBN 978-1-55152-632-4
(html)

    1. Adoptive parents. 2. Parenting. 3. Adopted children—
Psychology. 4. Adoption—Psychological aspects. I. Title.

HV875.C763 2016   649'.145   C2015-908282-X
                                            C2015-908283-8

To all my children in gratitude for
all they have taught me

Adopting

It was supposed to be simple
Easy to love with my heart so full
But perhaps not so easy for my sons
Who rocked with a sudden shock to trust
Not felt by me.
It was an underground shift
A shudder felt later, much later.
For some, that shift trembles for decades.
For others, a ripple that disappears
Below my senses.
I happily assumed no fault line.
Ignorance is not helpful.
It is better to be alert to seismology
Of the sliding yet to come.
Better to build a house of love, strong and flexible, capable of
    movement
That can rock with the tremors and sudden quakes at the
    foundation
Than wonder why our children
Are dancing, twisting, striving to fly
Unaware they are trying to keep their balance
On the rolling earth beneath them.

Contents

Thicker Than Blood

Acknowledgments

My thanks to the over fifty young people who gave me their time and their information in my research. I agreed not to publish their names and so cannot thank them individually.

Thanks also to the Adoptive Families Association of British Columbia, in particular Karen Madeiros, Mary Caros, and Brianna Brash-Nyberg. Thanks to Adam Pertman of the National Center of Adoption and Permanency for his encouragement. Dan Grant, Senior Planner (Retired), Citizenship & Immigration Canada, the collector of my extensive family history, and the adoptive parent of two now-adult children, read the manuscript and gave me valuable advice. Dennis Emmett, retired elementary school principal and adoptive parent of two, read the manuscript for relevance. Jill Brandon, my beta-reader, read for content and had an eagle eye for spelling. Nancy Nelson generously added her experience as a foster parent. I am grateful to my sons who added their perspective as adoptees and to Dean Fortin who also gave me information on what it is like to be an adult adoptee.

My previous book *The Face in the Mirror: Teens and Adoption* gave the perspective of teen adoptees on their experience. In this book, I have added the retrospective thoughts of adult adoptees on what would have helped them and their adoptive parents navigate the sometimes difficult waters of their relationships. This book was built in part on the knowledge I gained from the many people who contributed to the earlier book and to the insight and ideas of those who live in the adoption world at some point of the constellation. My thanks to the many passionate people I met at conferences and meetings during the research stage of this book who talked about their adoption experiences and encouraged my writing.

Foreword

Adam Pertman

The phone conversation took place over two decades ago, but I can still hear my mother's words as clearly as if she'd spoken them yesterday. I had called to tell her that, minutes earlier, my wife and I had received the exhilarating, exquisite news that a boy had been born in Colorado and his mother had chosen us to become his adoptive parents. "Mazel tov, that's so wonderful," my mother said, her smile so penetrating that it was almost audible. Then, lovingly, almost incidentally, she offered a bit of wisdom that has stayed with me ever since. "All right," she said. "Now you can worry for the rest of your life."

Nearly all parents, regardless of how we become parents, experience the poignant truth of my mother's insight—from the time we begin worrying about our children's health and development as infants, through the continuum of anxiety about their conduct and performance during their school years, and finally, into our ongoing concern about their careers and relationships once they become adults. The complicated truth is that, among the many positive and negative behaviours children induce in their parents, one is (usually) unambiguously wonderful: perpetual, selfless concern for another human being.

At a time when adoption is increasingly normalized throughout North America—certainly more so on this continent than any other—most people have come to understand that parents through adoption are mainly just plain parents, with the same day-to-day feelings, tasks, and responsibilities as parents through in-vitro fertilization;

parents through sperm or egg "donation" (in quotes because the "donors" of the gametes are usually paid, but that's another conversation); parents through remarriage; parents through the tried-and-true, broken-condom approach; single and gay and lesbian and kinship and divorced and guardianship and foster parents; and so on. All parents. In so many ways, probably most ways, all the same. And all very, very different, with unique characteristics and challenges and realities.

It's important to understand the differences among the many types of contemporary families, or at least have a strong sense of them, because otherwise we risk falling into the trap of judging which are better or worse—and that judgment can translate into derogatory language, condescending attitudes, and hurtful actions. As recently as the middle of the last century, for instance, society stigmatized divorce and (I'm exaggerating just a little to make the point) wondered how children could survive the experience; no one now says divorce is a good thing, but we generally recognize its realities and don't systemically malign those affected by it. Similarly, some people still believe there shouldn't be single or LGBT parents, primarily because the children ostensibly suffer damaging consequences; research and experience tell a very different story, of course, and so single-parent families are already broadly accepted and, by historical standards, LGBT-led families are getting there at lightning speed, accelerated by the legalization of same-sex marriage.

So, how does adoption fit into this picture? As I mentioned a couple of paragraphs ago, the institution is more normalized than it has ever been. That doesn't mean, however, that its participants finally function on a level playing field with members of biologically formed families. Indeed, adopted people throughout North America, even as adults, face inequities and indignities such as being prohibited from obtaining their own birth certificates; first/birth mothers continue to be shamed, disrespected, and driven underground; adoptive parents continue to receive unwelcome sympathy because they couldn't have "real children" (you should see my son and daughter—they look real); and the words "you're adopted," incredibly, are still sometimes used as an insult. Like many of the varied family types I listed above, adoption still has a long way to go to achieve genuine legal and cultural parity. That's why *Thicker than Blood* is so timely and important. Within a genre that consists primarily of how-tos, memoirs, and explorations of specific issues—single parenting, LGBT families, etc.—Marion Crook's new book is broad, complex, and ambitious. It's also insightful, well-crafted and even humorous at times, all testaments to the author's experience and skill as a researcher/writer. But none of those attributes would elevate *Thicker than Blood* above the pack were it not for the book's scope, its ability to pull together history, sociology, psychology, and people's real-life stories—including Crook's own—in order to educate readers about the realities of adoption and of everyone that the institution envelops. We come away understanding that families are fundamentally the same, and fundamentally different. To quote a line from my own book, *Adoption Nation:* "Different isn't better or worse, it's just different."

That's an important lesson—and, again, it's why *Thicker than Blood* is the right book at the right time—not just for Canadians and Americans for whom adoption is a palpable part of everyday life, but also for anyone who interacts with those tens of millions of adoptees, first/birth parents, adoptive parents, and other relatives—yes, really, tens of millions—as well as for anyone who simply wants to better understand our increasingly diverse, inclusive world.

Adam Pertman is President and Founder of the National Center on Adoption and Permanency and the author of *Adoption Nation: How the Adoption Revolution is Transforming Our Families and America.* *nationalcenteronadoptionandpermanency.net*

Introduction

My adopted sons were in their early teen years when I realized I was floundering in ignorance about adoption. No one was writing about teens—there were books about preschoolers and middle-school adoptees, but nothing about parenting adopted teens. I complained about this to a publisher at a book-trade fair in Toronto. She had recently commissioned a book on adoption for middle-school children. I said that a book for teens was more urgently needed, and she offered me a contract to write one. I had to stop complaining and get busy, so I plunged into the world of teenaged adoptees.

With my youngest child who was then thirteen and his friend of the same age, and a very pregnant friend and her toddler, I headed east, stopping in cities along the way to talk to teens about adoption. When we arrived in Winnipeg, I found that a friend there had put an ad in the paper with her phone number as a contact. The phone rang for hours. I couldn't meet with all the teens who called and wanted to be interviewed. However, I continued to interview teens using the ad-in-the-paper method in other cities, and by the publication of the second edition of my book *The Face in the Mirror: Teens and Adoption* (Arsenal Pulp Press, 2000), I had interviewed fifty teenagers. I learned what teens thought about adoption, especially about the need for openness and honesty.

I continued to talk about teens and adoption for many years

while I adjusted to big changes in my own life—divorce, grown children, the rigorous work of obtaining my PhD from the University of British Columbia, and then establishing my life as an academic. When I left academia, I returned to writing. The world of adoption had changed; I wanted to understand it. It's easier to be wise about our children if we have a broad understanding of many children, particularly those who have the same concerns as ours. Most of us don't have time to attend child psychology classes and get our education from books, workshops, and in conversations with others. Without a lot of spare time, we need a resource that's quick to read, doesn't require a dictionary, and helps us reflect on our own situation. We pick up information while waiting for a bus, at the dentist's office, or parked outside the school. Adoptive parents need a book that contains a broad and modern view of adoption. I couldn't find that book, so I wrote *Thicker than Blood*. I didn't envision it as one of instruction, but rather as a conversation about what I've learned and experienced, in the hope that readers can agree, disagree, consider, and adopt what is here and adapt it to their lives.

There have been huge changes for adoptive parents over the past thirty years. Instead of the standard closed adoptions of the past where birth parents and adoptive parents were hidden from each other, most adoptions now are open. Birth parents and adoptive parents at least know one another's names. Following the 1970s, few babies were available for adoption domestically in North America, so in the '80s until about 2004, many adoptive parents looked to international sites for children. Transracial adoptions became much more common and still occur, although at a much lower rate, and foster parent adoptions also became possible. Adoptive families and foster families used to be separate entities; now there is less separation, as more children are adopted from foster care. The new openness in adoption also included surrogate mothers and progenitors who donated eggs or sperm for in-vitro fertilizations; "parents" is now an inclusive term.

With the demise of secrecy, closer cultural affiliation between adopted Native children and members of Native bands is more possible today. The goal is no longer to assimilate Native children into white society, denying them their cultural affiliations. Adoptive parents of these children are now educated to see the value of close contact with Native communities. Differences of race are less likely denied and more likely celebrated.

Some reprehensible practices are still with us. People continue to buy and sell babies in the black market. There are still baby brokers in many states. Children are offered for "re-homing" on Craigslist. Organizations still send planeloads of children from one country to another to find safe homes for them but without considering their individual needs or even if they have been freely relinquished. In some countries, poverty is so dire that women and girls are pressured into selling their babies. Denmark has prohibited adoptions from Nigeria because "baby factories" there were housing pregnant young women and selling their children in the adoption "market."[1] Treating children as commodities is not restricted to the past.

Recent Research

Dan Siegel, professor of clinical psychiatry at the UCLA School of Medicine and executive director of the Mindsight Institute, suggests that nurture can influence biology; parents can influence their children's biological patterns even after birth. This melding of biological and social science fascinates me. Siegel suggests that quantum physics might explain how the trauma of separation, neglect, and abuse can change brain patterns. We all try to make sense of our lives, and we need to help our children make sense of theirs.

Adam Pertman, president and CEO of the National Center on Adoption and Permanency, intrigued me with his new vision of success and permanency. He is a respected researcher and journalist who has a philosophical approach grounded in research. He asks parents to consider how we can create the attitudes and policies we need so that every child can have a permanent and successful home. If we first alter our philosophy of adoption, we may also be able to alter governmental and organizational policies and practices.

I enjoyed reading the scholarly overview of adoption by Michael Grand, professor of Clinical Child Psychology at the University of Guelph, and the practical guide to transracial parenting by Beth Hall and Gail Steinberg in *Inside Transracial Adoption*. I attended a workshop that Hall gave on the subject and found that my experience as a mother in an transracial family was validated. Maris Blechner, a New York adoption consultant, asked workshop participants to consider the consumer nature of adoption; that is, the push for a "perfect" family and the "return if broken" thinking of so many of today's adults, including adoptive parents. In the field of adoption, we all rely on the work of David Kirk (who advised me to get my doctorate) and Nancy Verrier, who wrote about separation trauma, those activist groups who pushed for attention to the "Sixties Scoop" and "black homes for black babies," and the many groups who influenced the adoption of children into a different-race family.

I love the opportunities provided by webinars (online educational sessions) that are periodically offered by adoptive parents' associations. I find it efficient to sit in my study, log onto a webinar, and get the latest information from either my local association or a national one presented by an expert in the field. I have taken webinars by Lori Holden, Andrea Chatwin, Beth Hall, and Dr Anne Clayton. I feel connected to people in the world of adoption who also look for continuing education and, conveniently, can get it online.

I attended the North American Council on Adoptable Children Conference in Los Angeles in 2015 and was one of over 900 people who were determined to create loving families. There are conferences across Canada and the US whose sole aim is to improve the lives of children. It's emotionally satisfying to be around so many people who share that goal.

From conversations on Internet sites and with attendees at conferences and workshops, I am aware of researchers and writers in this field who work with passion and conviction to create a greater understanding of how adoption affects our children. There are more researchers and activists in the field than ever before, and more changes and new possibilities than I had imagined.

Wars, famines, and poverty in many parts of the world create a huge need for homes for displaced children. But even if the world was an ideal place with adequate health and social care, there would still be children available for adoption. Disasters and death happen to birth parents, and their children need permanent homes. Birth parents abandoned by their own parents feel incapable of raising children, and look for a safe place for them.

The transfer of children from birth to adoptive family is accompanied, to a greater or lesser extent, by emotional trauma. Adoptive parents need to learn how to mitigate that trauma. This is not a child-raising skill we acquire from our parents; it is a skill we need to learn. As they grow through the teen years and into young adulthood, adopted children also go through identity challenges that we did not experience, so we need to learn how best to help them.

We open our homes and hearts to children who need us. There are singles and couples who want the experience of family and who have love to share. We have tried to raise healthy and happy children, but today, with increased knowledge around adoption, we can do a better job. This book is my contribution to that increasing knowledge.

1   "Denmark Bans Nigeria Adoptions after Raid on Suspected Baby Factory," The Guardian, April 30, 2014. http://www.theguardian.com/global-development/2014/apr/30/denmarks-bans-nigerian-adoption-raid-baby-factory

A Note on Terms

A broader view of adoption brings changes in terminology. I understand that some birth mothers prefer to be called "first mothers" or simply "mothers"—because they *are* mothers. I respect their right to choose their title, but I needed to be clear about who is being referred to in the book and so chose to use the term "birth mothers." Adoptive parents may prefer to be called simply "parents." I prefer this myself, but I will use "adoptive parents" in the text so that readers know which parents I mean. In my first book, I avoided the word "adoptee" and said "someone who had been adopted." I have grown past the notion that adoption was left in the past and now accept that adoptees need to integrate past experiences into the present. They are *always* adoptees, however deeply they are loved and a part of their adoptive families. Acceptance of this term contributes to understanding the adoptee's point of view. Language exposes culture, and the use of modern terms around adoption shows an increasing understanding of the adoption process.

There is some confusion around the words "transracial" and "interracial." We hear them used interchangeably at times. "Trans" means across and "inter" means between. Here I use "transracial" when discussing children in families across all relationships in a family and "interracial" when discussing marriage between two people.

Secrecy in Adoption

We come to adoption today convinced that the more we know about our children's birth family, the better we will be able to support and guide them. We work hard at finding ways to support membership in their first family while firmly establishing them in our adoptive family. We see secrecy as somehow dishonest—and the children also see it that way, as the teens I interviewed told me.[1] They couldn't understand why their adoptive parents, chiefly their mothers, didn't tell them that they were adopted. It seemed a betrayal of their relationship. This is unlikely to happen now, but it used to be common. If your birth is hidden, then it must be shameful.

By trying to maintain secrecy, adoptive families can perpetrate denial and false narratives. We don't plan it that way; and we don't necessarily want it that way, but because of social agency practices and state and provincial laws, we can find ourselves telling awkward family stories that are fictional. We are real families and we deserve real stories.

Pre-1900s

It was not always possible to hide the act of adoption. In Native cultures, adoption by relatives was obvious and continues to be so today in many tribal communities.

"He's my cousin," an Inuit teen told me. "Actually, he's my brother but my aunt and uncle adopted him, so he's my cousin."

It was clear to her and to him. Nothing complicated there.

My own family, which is tribal and prolific (I have sixty first cousins), came from Scotland and has an ancient history of adoption. The head of our clan in the fourteenth century was an adopted son called "Young Mackinnon." He inherited a castle and a great amount of land in the Hebrides which, unfortunately for me and my cousins, was lost and is now a pile of rubble on a promontory. Adoption was part of clan life. In tribal societies, there was no secret about who the child was and where he or she had come from. There was a practical connection between mother and child. Someone had to breastfeed the child, so secrecy was unlikely.

If we had retained the clan system, adopted children would likely know who their birth parents were and how they came to be in their adoptive family. But the British legal system, which forms the basis of our North American law, did not recognize children's needs as important—they did, after all, send eight-year-olds into the mines. Both adopted and biological children had few rights. Children were often used as labour and beaten with impunity. Violence toward children was simply considered discipline.

For many years there was no legal adoption system, so "inconvenient" children landed in neighbouring homes, the families of relatives, or orphanages. The system of informal adoption (sometimes called "custom" adoption) occurs in some societies today and, while often practical, can be unnerving for adoptive families who fear birth parents might exert a legal right and "reclaim" the child. If enough social pressure is in place in a tribe or clan this will not happen, but the threat alone can be daunting.

In 1762, Jean-Jacques Rousseau wrote his book *Emile, or On Education*. Ironically, Rousseau placed all five of his children in orphanages where, in the conditions of those times, they surely died; he never raised any of them. He was one of the world's worst hypocrites, but he was such a compelling writer that he became an expert in children's education. He professed that children were born "good"—a revolutionary idea contrary to the church's teaching that all were born "wicked."[2] As a result of his writings, people began to consider children, particularly orphans, as vulnerable members of society and in need of rescue.[3]

Some English philanthropic societies organized "care," the kind they thought appropriate, which would get orphans from the towns and lift the burden on the parish to feed and house them. The first documented boatload of orphans was sent from England to the New World of Richmond, Virginia, in 1618. Over the following 350 years, 150,000 children were transported to the colonies.[4] They were not always orphans; their parents had not always given consent; and they were not all adopted. Many were spirited away and used as servants and labourers.[5] Even when laws permitted it, few of these children were adopted. Their best interests were not served, and their origins were considered irrelevant.[6]

This was not true in all cases, and some adopted children were considered important members of society. Legal contracts were drawn up between biological and adoptive parents. Jane Austen's brother Edward, for example, was adopted at the age of fifteen by his wealthy aunt and uncle who had no heir and who seemed motivated by love and affection for the whole family.[7] His adoption secured him a position he would not have had otherwise in late-eighteenth century society; his birth parents were well-known and socially accepted—just not rich. His adoption would have been publically acknowledged. In Edward's case, wealth was added to respectability.

The poor were another matter. Canada was created in 1867 by a confederation of French, English, and Indigenous peoples in part to prevent annexation by the US. It was a land of opportunity, especially for those from the British Isles. In the mid-nineteenth century, Maria Rye (English) and Annie McPherson (Scottish) set up a business transporting British orphans to Canada[8] and successfully ran a child-transportation business that netted them a tidy profit. When an inspector from the British government investigated their business in 1874, he found that while Rye and McPherson were motivated by Christian charity, they were also naïve. The children were often mistreated and, once placed, were abandoned by Rye and McPherson, who did not check up on them.

Collective public attitudes of philanthropy and care were often countered by individual tolerance of child abuse and maltreatment. Children were, generally, not considered socially valuable. Between 1870 and 1925, approximately twenty-five British organizations sent children to Canada. The background of those children, while not a secret, was not considered important or even documented. A child's history was whatever he or she remembered from the past.

Charles Loring Brace, a Protestant minister, was also in the business of transporting children, but he was apparently motivated by philanthropy. He helped to establish The Children's Aid Society of New York to improve life for children of the poor.[9] Between 1854 and 1929, The Children's Aid Society moved over 100,000 children—called orphans, but not necessarily so—from the streets of New York City to homes across the US. Some of the children were adopted into families, but many were simply used as child labour. The question was not whether to adopt but how hard they could work. There was no attempt to perpetuate secrecy about the child's beginnings, just the attitude that their original families were best forgotten. And since neither their first families nor The Children's Aid Society checked on them, some were mistreated.[10]

I have tried to imagine what the societal attitude toward

children must have been to allow cruelties to be condoned on such a scale. Tolerance of physical abuse was systemic. I can remember a time in my own early childhood when teachers, neighbours, and total strangers could smack a child without repercussions; children were considered half-savage and in need of discipline. There are still people who think hitting children is justified by the anger, frustration, or need for power felt by the adult. The difference is that today we aren't quite so willing to accept that behaviour as normal—or legal.

The British child migrant system took 500,000 children to Australia from the 1940s until the 1990s.[11] The horror stories these children told later of abuse at the hands of the religious Brothers and the adoptive families were sickening, and the Australian government issued a public apology to them in 2009.[12] The United Kingdom apologized to former child migrants and their families in 2010.[13] Canada refused to apologize,[14] although documented accounts of abuse of children from the migrant programs are public knowledge and a public shame.

Not everyone was a monster, of course. Many people were philanthropic and well-intentioned. In England, there were organizations such as the National Child Adoption Association, founded in 1917, that worked to provide the best homes for children and supported regulatory adoption laws. In the US the first such laws were passed in Massachusetts in 1851.[15] Slow to follow suit, Canada passed its first adoption law in Ontario in 1921,[16] and England passed its initial adoption law in 1926.[17] The laws varied in the rights and responsibilities they outlined, but by the 1930s most western countries were committed to legal and regulated placement of children and to keeping their origins a secret. The notion that a child's past and heredity were best forgotten meant that non-identifying information was passed on to both parties, but it could be and sometimes was (as I found out in my research with teens) fictitious.

The Twentieth Century
1900–30

The use of infant formula became more available. Until the 1920s, the adoption of infants was not practical unless the family could find and afford a wet nurse. After the development of formula that was more nutritious, infants could be placed at birth into a family, and the family could pretend the child was born to them. The substitute child arrived in the family as if born to it, and the secrecy around the birth of an adopted child wormed its way into government and adoption agency policies.

Adoptive families sometimes pretended that the child was born to the parents. The mother discreetly retired to a "spa" for a few months and returned with a baby. Or the family did not discuss the child's origins at all, and consequently, others kept quiet about it. Secrecy around adoption came with the firmly held notion that the families of origin were of a lesser social class than adoptive families. Popular opinion held that illegitimate children were born only to the lower classes. Adoption implied illegitimacy, which meant lower-class, despite evidence to the contrary. People conveniently ignored the "early" babies and private adoptions of relatives in their own class. The strictures on early twentieth-century women to remain virgins until married required that illegitimate births be hidden to protect the mother's social standing. In order to hide "illegitimacy," the children had to be seen as both nameless and without family at birth. Secrecy and its accompanying emotional scarring became entrenched in the adoption process

The notion that an adopted child was either of a lower class or tainted in some way by illegitimacy was strong enough to sway intelligent people and support social policy. In England, and to some extent in Commonwealth countries, social class was inherited and only legitimate blood children had a right to their class. As if raising pedigreed horses, society had to know the blood lines. To adopt a child from a lower class meant risking all the problems of the lower class, a view which has persisted with surprising tenacity to the present time. "Bad blood"—that is, the blood of the poor—seemed to carry moral weaknesses, so adoption needed to be hidden, particularly if the adoptee was not a relative.

In the US, the land of opportunity, where "every child can become President," that attitude should have been ridiculed as it was not consistent with the notion of equality. But American society did not repudiate it, and accepted the notion that adopted children were "lower class" for many years.

The purpose of adoption laws during the early part of the century was not simply to give adopted children the right to inherit and adoptive parents the right to give property to their adopted children, but also to provide a good home to the children. Permanent homes were necessary for a child's and adoptive family's sense of security. Adoption laws protected children from being picked up by biological families like pets that are boarded for a time. Because adoption was often a secret, adoptive parents looked for children who looked like them. Agencies in North America sought out children to "match" the adoptive parents; the needs of the adoptive parents were paramount.

The ongoing secrecy

By the 1930s and '40s in North America, identifying information about birth parents and adoptive parents was screened by governmental bureaucracy. Social workers became powerful gatekeepers.

The original notion of privacy and confidentiality around adoption served the idea that the child should be protected from being branded as illegitimate—a social stigma that was real and disenfranchising at the time. As well, confidentiality laws protected adoptive parents from being harassed or blackmailed by unscrupulous birth parents. There were very likely a few instances of this, but all birth parents were blocked from knowing where their children were placed. Psychologists, social workers, and others believed it was in the best interests of the children and adoptive parents to deny a child's birth parents, family, and situation in order to create a new life for the child. The birth mother was without rights. While the child's sense of a secure home was part of the rationalization for this, an amazing amount of hubris, a belief in the superiority of the adoptive family, went into this attitude. A friend of mine who was born in 1942 told me she was well into her forties before she learned that the woman she thought of as her sister was biologically her cousin, the daughter of her mother's sister.

During and immediately after World War II, many more babies became available for adoption. Brief encounters, the desperate intimacy of the war years, and the difficulty of accessing birth control or abortion had produced many babies without families to care for them.

The 1950s

During the 1950s, while an increasing number of babies were being placed for adoption, Jean Paton wrote a book, *The Adopted Break Silence*,[18] in which she related her own experience as an adopted child and put forward the notion that adopted children should know who their birth parents were and thereby know their connection to humanity. She established a reunion organization called Orphan Voyage and began a movement that advocated the right of adopted children to find their biological families. It is now hard to imagine how restricted and stymied an adoptee in the pre-Internet era could be when looking for information about their family of origin. There were many gatekeepers: doctors, hospital staff, social workers, and adoptive parents and their relatives. Most people in those days did not believe that the adoptee had a right to the information. Babies were seen as a blank slate, with no emotional lives before they were born. Adoptees should be convinced that their adoptive parents were their only familial bond. Therefore there was no need, in the eyes of the gatekeepers, for the adoptees to be informed about their origins. It took many years before those gatekeepers recognized the validity of the adoptees' search. Adoptees tried many tactics to find their birth families. I imagine others might have developed the talent of one of the teens I interviewed. She could furtively read the official papers on the social worker's desk upside down, without the social worker knowing. Pregnant, young unmarried women were often sent away from home to live with relatives or in religious institutions to have their babies. The babies were taken from them, sometimes against their wishes, and placed for adoption. A markedly dreadful institution of this kind was the Ideal Maternity Home in Nova Scotia, the infamous "Butterbox" institution, where healthy babies were sold to adoptive homes, but sick ones were allowed to die and then buried in the butter boxes from the local dairy.[19]

The civil rights movement of the 1950s in the US increased awareness of racial inequality, chiefly for black people, and the swell of indignation against that inequality influenced adoption policies. The notion that "all are equal" promoted transrracial adoptions, although the "custom" adoption in Native groups and within the black communities of the US were not recognized by law. Until now, white communities had been willing to let non-white communities adopt their own children. Now, with increased awareness of equality, all children began to be eligible for adoption, particularly by white families. Both American and Canadian adoption agencies increased the number of placements of Native children and other children of colour with white families. Some US states removed laws that had prohibited transracial adoptions.[20] Coincidentally, with the availability of birth control, fewer white babies were available for adoption. So, with practical, altruistic, and sometimes shameful motives, the "Sixties Scoop" of Native children and an increased placement of black children in non-black homes began.[21]

The 1960s

THE RESISTANCE IN BLACK COMMUNITIES

Prior to the 1950s, black children were not often placed in white homes, but by 1967 there was a concerted effort by adoption agencies to change this practice, and an increasing number of Asian, black, and Native children were placed with white families.[22] The children were often denied affiliation with their family of origin. In 1972, acting as representatives of black communities in the US, the National Association of Black Social Workers objected to the placement of black children in white homes for much the same reasons as Aboriginal people did.[23] They cited difficult psychological adjustments and asserted that children of colour placed in white families had trouble establishing their identity. The children did not know who they were. As a consequence of these efforts, most adoption agencies now try to place children in a family of their own race, though children are still placed transracially. This does not mean racially diverse families are second-rate, but it does mean adoptive parents must be more aware of the importance of race. Parents today realize race plays an important part in a child's life, more intensely during the teen and young adult years.

> When he was six, I escorted my son through the Royal British Columbia Museum, conscientiously pointing out the many Tsimshian artifacts—masks, bowls, cloaks. This was when we thought he was Tsimshian.
>
> He studied the displays and turned to me. "How come there's so much of us here, Mom?"
>
> I was stunned speechless for a moment. He identified with being Tsimshian, but in his six-year-old mind, that meant I was Tsimshian too. What could I say that would support his identity as a Tsimshian boy without alienating him from me?
>
> I said, "We were good artists." I'd straighten it out when he was twelve.

Adopted children accepted by their adoptive families may not understand the significance of race in their lives until they are well into their teen years when they hit the prejudices of the larger social world—though some are aware of it very early, especially if their adoptive parents point it out. Establishing identity is difficult in a family where the adopted children look different from their parents or siblings. Not impossible, but difficult.

The sixties scoop

In Canada and the US, poverty, prejudice, and disenfranchisement resulted in difficult lives for the children of the poor, particularly the poor on Native reserves and reservations. The social agencies of these countries responded by ignoring custom adoption processes and rounding up the children, displacing them by the carload—and sometimes by the busload—from their home communities to adoptive or foster homes across the country and into other countries. Britain received planeloads of Aboriginal children from

Canada in the 1960s, and many Aboriginal children were taken from Canada between 1958 and 1967 by the Indian Adoption Project of the Bureau of Indian Affairs and the Child Welfare League of America in the US.[24] The parents of these children, assumed to be uncaring, were often coerced into giving their children away. At times, the children were taken by the agencies when their parents were sick in hospital or away gathering supplies. There are many stories of social workers telling the parents that they were taking the children "for now, while you are sick" and never returning them.[25] This was part of an inexplicable assumption of the superiority of the white race, in spite of the protests of Native people and the tenets of the civil rights movement. The adoption workers held an unexamined belief that the children would have better lives away from their families.

To be fair, placement of Native children in non-Native homes meant, in many instances, that the children grew up in loving adoptive families.[26] Some birth mothers voluntarily placed their children in non-Native families, but many did not. Individual success stories do not negate the devastation these social policies conferred on many Native children.

Unstated was the notion that Native people would be assimilated into white society and eventually their culture would disappear. The parents often did not give consent, or they were tricked into signing consent forms. According to stories in Suzanne Fournier and Ernie Crey's book *Stolen from Our Embrace*, some social workers driving the "Sixties Scoop" enthusiastically stripped entire villages of most of the children, separated them, and sent them into foster care. "Abduction of Aboriginal children has persisted long past that decade [the sixties]," write Fournier and Crey. "By the late 1970s, one in four status Indian children could expect to be separated from his or her parents for all or part of childhood."[27] Decades of systematic child abductions have created horrendous cultural problems, and Aboriginal children continue to be overrepresented in apprehension statistics. Adoptive parents often did not know the particulars of the apprehension. Social workers created an acceptable story, and adoptive parents believed it. It was only years later that many adoptive parents realized they had participated in the Scoop.

Residential Schools for Native Children

In Canada, church-run residential schools, which thousands of Native children were forced to attend in the nineteenth and twentieth centuries, robbed Natives of the experience of being in a family and left many incapable of parenting because they had lived only in institutional environments, with no models of how to parent. Instead of addressing their need to learn parenting skills, social agencies removed the children of those who'd been raised in residential schools; this perpetuated the problem by separating these children from their families and culture. It has taken fifty years to reveal the effects of this practice, and the consequences are likely to challenge generations to come.

The resistance to transracial adoption

In British Columbia between 1961 and 1971, agencies placed many more Native children in non-Native homes than they had before. Protest grew in Aboriginal communities. In 1973, in response to pressure from Aboriginal communities and organizations, the British Columbia provincial government put a moratorium on the adoption of Native children by non-Native families. Aboriginal people feared a continuation of the "Sixties Scoop."

This was a personal disaster for my family. There we were, with our Aboriginal son, a delightful and loving guy, with a moratorium on his adoption. I felt like a she-bear defending her cub. I didn't care about politics and societal attitudes. I wanted him protected by law. My family had asked for a baby, and the social welfare agency had placed him with us, asking if it was okay if he was Native. We said, "Sure." We didn't have much awareness or do much planning around the fact that he was a Native boy in a white family, but he had taken over our hearts. We *were* a family. I stormed off to the offices of the Union of British Columbia Indian Chiefs and had a heart-to-heart with the representative there. He calmed me down. I had no idea we were part of the "Sixties Scoop." He understood that and explained that the Aboriginal bands in my province had no intention of pulling the children from their current homes and planned to leave them with their adoptive parents, but they wanted to prevent other similar adoptions. This moratorium forced a change in attitude around the placement of Native children. At three, my son's adoption went through. I began to understand his affiliation with Aboriginal communities, my unwitting participation in the Scoop, and his place in our family. It was and continues to be complicated.

Increasing demands for "Indian homes for Indian children" were made by the Adoption Resource Exchange of North America at the same time adoption agencies were sending Native children out of the area and even out of the country.[28] In 1979, 339 children, many of whom were Native, were sent from Canada to the US for adoption because Native children could move across the border without legal hindrance (under the Jay Treaty).[29] This situation was astounding and horrifying to Native peoples. Because adoption processes during the 1950s to '70s were essentially secretive or closed, the Native children lost their sense of belonging to their own tribe or clan.

A child's history given to the adoptive parents may be wrong.

Many times, the birth story the social worker provided to the adoptive families was a fantasy. We were told my son belonged to the Tsimshian Nation. Not true. After twenty years, we found he was actually a member of the Gitxsan Nation—a neighbouring nation, but different. It was like being told he was Apache and finding out he was Hopi, or being told he was Scottish and finding out he was English. Definitely not the same thing. It seemed disrespectful on the part of the social workers, and it angered me when I discovered we had all been lied to. I threw things.

"Hey, Mom," my son said. "It's not such a big deal." But it was, and I knew it was.

Accuracy in the adoptee's history wasn't important then to social agencies. It wasn't until much later that children's right to know their origins became vital. Certainly there was little attempt by social agencies to support the adoptive parents' attempts to foster affiliations with the child's culture.

Most Native communities in the US and Canada are clusters of family constellations that have endured for centuries. Every child has a place and is valued as a member of a family cluster. Adopting the child out does not change this; that place remains his or hers. Children are valued because they are members of families. Losing the children to non-Native homes, especially in such great numbers, caused not only emotional pain for those involved, but huge problems for those seeking family reunification and tribal affiliations. In an effort to reverse this drain of children away from their home communities, Aboriginal associations demanded—and are still demanding—Native homes for Native children. The system isn't perfect. There are many Native children who cannot find Native homes, but the social agencies of the tribal communities are increasingly more efficient and effective and do grant exceptions so some children can be placed in non-Native families.

MATCHING CHILDREN TO PARENTS

By the mid-1970s, the number of babies available for adoption in Western countries had been reduced substantially due to increasingly effective birth control, career women waiting longer to have children, the legalization of abortion, and a reduction of the stigma of illegitimacy, so more single mothers kept their babies. The philosophy and practice moved from placing children in order to meet the needs of adoptive families to selecting families to meet the needs of the adoptable children—a paradigm shift that affected adoptive parents drastically. When the scarcity of adoptable children became obvious, families who wanted to adopt included couples who were infertile, couples who were fertile but chose to adopt, those who already had biological children, single men and women, and LGBTQ singles and couples. There was a greater diversity of adoptive families or at least a greater frankness about that diversity. Because infants were difficult to find, these families began to look across national borders for children. People who had previously not considered children of other races and "special" children, those with physical and psychological needs, were now more open to adopting them. The fantasy of the "matched" family began to fracture when more and more families now looked different, not just in hair colour and physical features, but in skin colour. Such an obvious difference advertised adoption, and adoptive families began to find the concept of secrecy somewhat absurd.

THE RIGHT TO KNOW

With this new attitude toward frankness within the family, parents were advised to tell their children at a very early age that they had been adopted. When children were *not* told and discovered as teens they were adopted (and somehow they did discover this), they felt betrayed and lied to by their birth parents, principally by their birth mothers.[30] The lie was considered to be more detrimental to the children's mental health than the fact of adoption.

"How could she lie to me?" a teen I interviewed told me. "She was supposed to be my mother. What kind of mother lies to her daughter?"

It was hard for me to answer except to say her adoptive mother hadn't had good advice. As the children who had been adopted in the age of closed adoptions grew up, they began to vigorously protest against the former secrecy and organize advocacy groups, agitating for their right to know their heritage. In response, many institutions—not without protest from threatened adoptive parents—began to demand the laws be changed to accommodate the adoptees' demands. Established in Britain and then in North America, the changes in legislation gradually made it easier for adoptees to find their birth parents. As well, biological fathers began to demand rights they hadn't had in the past so they could look for their lost children. This can still be difficult, but is more possible than in the past.[31] Adoptees could register at a central agency and find birth parents. The need to know one's biological roots began to seem legitimate, especially when it was expressed by adopted adults who had very strong ties with their adoptive families and who appeared to have rational and valid reasons for searching. Looking for birth families was not only for the abused, the disturbed, and the unstable; it was a genuine and common need.

The "need to know" became the "right to know" and shaped the idea of open adoption, which meant all parties—birth parents, adoptive parents, and adoptees—could know of each other. So we circle back to the ways of our ancestors when children were placed in homes where they could be cared for and everyone knew where the child was—and who he or she was. There is now choice at the time of adoption about how much knowledge and contact both sets of parents expect and what options they want for this child. Records are much more accessible. Permission to contact is often moot because the Internet makes investigating ancestry available to anyone who knows how to click and search. Biological parents can become Facebook friends.

The Twenty-first Century

The Internet makes it possible for children to search for their birth parents without the permission or knowledge of their adoptive parents. It's a huge step forward for many and the source of fear for some adoptive parents. There is some justification for their fears. Adoptees may search before they are ready to deal with rejection, because rejection by birth parents is a possibility. Since birth parents can also search for their children, adoptive parents may worry a birth parent will contact their child before that child is ready to handle the relationship. Not all birth parents or all adoptive parents are ideal.

Adoptive parents are forced to be frank with their children, more responsive to their needs, and to cooperative with birth parents. Secrecy seems impossible today, and the challenges of such open adoptions need to be discussed within the families.

It is now possible to find like-minded adoptees on the Internet. Finding fellow adoptees was much harder before the web revolutionized our world. Adoptees can read books such as *The Primal Wound* and *Attachment Disorders* and realize the problems discussed in these books are common to adoptees and are not a result of a personally haywired brain. It's some comfort. Most adoptees must deal with these issues. The lucky ones find insight, therapy, or coping skills that allow them to regulate that first emotional and physiological upheaval successfully, but many are overwhelmed by long-term effects.

The Internet allows adoptees to join with others to work at understanding and eventually dealing with their early trauma. Teen and adult adoptee groups encourage discussion. Adoptive parents can find others who are dealing with the same problems and receive advice and support. Organizations such as the Adoptive Families Association of British Columbia offer educational sessions, including webinars which allow parents to learn about some of the latest and most useful ideas around raising adopted kids. We are a long way from the lonely blundering we adoptive parents were forced to do in the days before what I call "enlightenment." Adoptive parenting is not the solitary and blindly intuitive process it was in the past. We tried to be honest, loving, and responsive to our kids without the knowledge and skills that present-day adoptive parents have. Today, adoptive parents are more able to get professional advice and help. Of course, it's not always easy.

The Importance of Love

Love is not mentioned in the adoption history books. You'd think the whole adoption process in the past was motivated solely by convenience, need, and duty. There must have been love, but you can't tell from the records. It would seem that a whole section on love in the adoption story of the past is missing. You will bump into my comments on love at the end of the chapters. Love does matter.

1   Marion Crook, *The Face in the Mirror: Teens and Adoption* (Vancouver: Arsenal Pulp Press, 2000).

2   Maurice Cranston, *The Noble Savage* (Chicago: University of Chicago Press, 1991).

3   Michele Erina Doyle and Mark K. Smith, "Jean-Jacques Rousseau on Education," *The Encyclopedia of Informal Education*, 2007. http://infed.org/thinkers/et-rous. htm.

4   "Child Migration History," Child Migrants Trust. [No date.] http://www.childmigrantstrust.com/our-work/child-migration-history

5   Nick Bryant, "Ordeal of Australia's Child Migrants," BBC News Australia, November 15, 2009. http://news.bbc.co.uk/2/hi/asia-pacific/8360150.stm

6   Eileen Fairweather, "Lost Children of the Empire." *MailOnLine*, December 10, 2009. http://www.dailymail.co.uk/news/article-1229776/

7   Park Honan, *Jane Austen: Her Life: The Definitive Portrait of Jane Austen: Her Life, Her Art, Her Family, Her World* (New York: Fawcett Columbine, 1987).

8   *"The Doyle Report on Pauper Children in Canada, February 1875."* http://canadianbritishhomechildren.weebly.com/the-doyle-report-1875.html

9   "History," The Children's Aid Society. [No date.] http://childrensaidsociety.org/ about/history

10   Lori Askeland, "Brace, Charles Loring (1826-1890)." *Encyclopedia of Children and Childhood in History and Society.* 2004. Encyclopedia.com. http://www.encyclopedia.com/doc/1G2-3402800072.html

11   Eileen Fairweather, "Lost Children of the Empire," *MailOnLine*, December 10, 2009. http://dailymail.co.uk/news/article-1229776/

12   "Apology to the Forgotten Australians and Former Child Migrants," Australian Government, Department of Social Services, March 30, 2015. https://www. dss.gov.au/our-responsibilities/families-and-children/programs-services/ apology-to-the-forgotten-australians-and-former-child-migrants

13   "Gordon Brown Apologises to Child Migrants Sent Abroad," BBC News, February 24, 2010. http://news.bbc.co.uk/2/hi/uk_news/8531664.stm

14   "Canada Doesn't Plan Child Migrant Apology," CBC News, November 16, 2009. http://www.cbc.ca/news/canada/canada-doesn-t-plan-child-migrant-apology-1.826140

15   Ellen Herman, "'Timeline on Adoption History,' The Adoption History Project," Department of History, University of Oregon. http://pages.uoregon.edu/ adoption/timeline.html

16   Anne Patterson, "Adoption in Ontario: A Brief History," Ontario GenWeb Resources. http://rootsweb.ancestry.com/~canon/research-topic-births-adoption. html

17　"Marriage: Legitimacy and Adoption," UK Parliament. http://www.parliament.
　　uk/about/living-heritage/transformingsociety/private-lives/relationships/
　　overview/legitimacyadoption/

18　Ellen Herman, "Jean Paton, The Adopted Break Silence." The Adoption History
　　Project, Department of History, University of Oregon. http://darkwing.uoregon.
　　edu/~adoption/archive/PatonTABS.htm

19　"'The Butterbox Babies Story," Canadian Children's Rights Council.http://
　　canadiancrc.com/Butterbox-Babies_Killers-Child-Trafficking-Canada/
　　Butterbox-Babies-Baby-killers-child-trafficking-selling-babies-Canada-adop-
　　tion-story.aspx

20　Ellen Herman, "Transracial Adoptions," The Adoption History Project,
　　Department of History, University of Oregon. http://pages.uoregon.edu/
　　adoption/topics/transracialadoption.htm Retrieved March 24, 2015.

21　Suzanne Fournier and Ernie Crey, *Stolen from Our Embrace: The Abduction of
　　First Nations Children and the Restoration of Aboriginal Communities.* (Vancouver :
　　Douglas & McIntyre, 1998.)

22　Deann Borshay Liem and NAATA, "Adoption History." *First Person Plural,*
　　December 2000. http://pbs.org/pov/firstpersonplural/history.php

23　"National Association of Black Social Workers, 'Position Statement on Trans-
　　Racial Adoption,' September 1972," The Adoptions History Project. [No date]
　　http://pages.uoregon.edu/adoption/archive/NabswTRA.htm

24　Margaret Ward, *The Adoption of Native Canadian Children* (Cobalt, ON:
　　Highway Book Shop, 1984.)

25　Fournier and Crey, *Stolen from Our Embrace.*

26　Cheryl Marlene Swidrovich, "Positive Experiences of First Nations Children in
　　Non-Aboriginal Foster or Adoptive Care: De-Constructing the 'Sixties Scoop.' A
　　thesis submitted to the College of Graduate Studies and Research." (Saskatoon,
　　SK: Native Studies, University of Saskatchewan, 2004.)

27　Fournier and Crey, *Stolen from Our Embrace.*

28　Karen Balcom, *The Traffic in Babies: Cross-border Adoption and Baby-selling
　　Between the United States and Canada, 1930-1972.* (Toronto, ON: University of
　　Toronto Press, 2011.)

29　"British-American Diplomacy. The Jay Treaty; November 19, 1794," The Avalon
　　Project: Documents in Law, History and Diplomacy, 2008. http://avalon.law.yale.
　　edu/18th_century/jay.asp and "Jay Treaty," *Wikipedia,* https://en.wikipedia.org/
　　wiki/Jay_Treaty

30　Crook, *The Face in the Mirror.*

31   Claudia Corrigan Darcy, "The Birth Fathers Rights in Adoption
      Relinquishment." *Musings of the Lame.* http://www.adoptionbirthmothers.com/
      fathers-rights-custody-adoption/

2 Why Parents Adopt

When I was young and adopting my first child, I rarely examined the motives behind my actions. Certainly, I didn't examine my motives for adoption. "My arms feel empty" was about as close as I got to self-analysis. My sister and sister-in-law had adopted children as had cousins on both sides of the family. Other parents stood in front of me at the adoption agency waiting for their babies. Adoption was not unusual. Now, on reflection, I can see that my motives, although unexamined at the time, were much the same as those who were in front and behind me in the adoption line and those who trundled through the hospital doors with their biological babies. I wanted a family.

The Need for Family

For the same reasons parents have biological children, we adopt. We want the experience of parenting; we want to create or expand our family, and we expect to have a richer, more rewarding life *because* we have a family. According to a recent survey, sixty-nine percent of adoptive parents have this motivation.[1] We joined the ranks of parents of all types who wanted children. There is nothing peculiar about us; we just want to create a family.

Being part of a family satisfies our need to belong, our need to accept a "tribal" affiliation that New Age proponents tell us is necessary for our emotional health.[2] Our Thanksgiving table needs to hold people we love as evidence that we belong. Few would argue affiliation wasn't important. Even in this era of individualization and declining social involvement,[3] we feel a strong need to connect with and build a family. We invest energy and time in this ideal and even sacrifice personal ambition for the good of the family. It is a simple concept and a powerful one, but so common that perhaps it is underappreciated. We expect to promote and defend our family. We expect to sacrifice for our children. We make the decision when we decide to have children, biological or adopted, that we will have less in our retirement fund because we must create an education fund, fewer trips to exotic places and more campouts. We'll have less time for painting and the symphony and more time for sixth-grade homework. Even in countries such as Denmark, where the government provides child care and quality education and pays tuition for university, parents still commit to years of child-first lives. Family is worth sacrificing for. The rewards are fulfilling.

Adoptive parents, like all parents, look for love and affection from their children and expect to give the same in return. We hope to have an emotionally rich life that includes interaction with our children.[4] Luckily, it is usually possible. Sometimes that emotional interaction includes anger, frustration, despair, heartbreak, worry, and helplessness—emotions most parents accept—along with joy, pride, satisfaction, amazement, stimulation, pleasure, happiness, fulfilment, and gratification. Children force change and reaction in the family. You know you've lived fully when children punctuate your life span with those emotions. Adoptive parents expect children to change our lives. We aren't necessarily prepared for how much they do this.

Altruism

Most of us respond to that pull of children who have no place to call their own. We have a strong desire to give a child a home. While this motive is often compelling, it is not necessarily altruistic because we know we are going to be amply rewarded by the bond we will create. Raising a child may not be easy, but we expect to gain emotional satisfaction, a response to our love and care, and a lifetime of involvement with our child.

Like the writer John M. Simmons (*The Marvelous Journey Home*), I am slightly repulsed by people who imply that because I have adopted children, I have a generous soul and have done something wonderful.[5] Of course, I responded to my children's need for a home, but I had selfish motives as well: I expected to receive joy, and I did. The notion of adoptive parents as saintly rescuers of the unfortunate makes me squirm as if someone was dressing me in a weird costume. I know there are those who believe they have been chosen by a higher power to save the homeless children of the world, but most of us, like parents of biological children, just want a family.

In Response to Social Influences

The motivations for adopting are varied. There seems to be a social context for motives, a sweeping feeling that is shared by many. In the 1960s, adoptive parents tended to have a romantic "as if born to" attitude. "She will be ours and we will love her. That's all she needs." It was the time of the idealized world of the hippies with the belief in love and good will to all. By the '80s young people had a more realistic view around the problems adopted children might face. They were aware that children had past lives, which likely would include trauma they had to deal with. There was less concern around the cost of adoption in those days, as much of

North America was still, for the most part, employed and optimistic. In the 2000s, a wave of altruism seemed to flood sectors of the community that saw adopting, in particular transracial and inter-country adoption, as a democratic ideal. Today adoptive parents live in a more individualistic society where they feel they have a right to a family and look to various ways to achieve it. It can be expensive, and parents want to know that the payment will result in an adoption.

However, we are not always or necessarily a product of our times.[6] Many people swim against the current, although we can be influenced by the cultural norms that surround us and our motivations can be influenced by them.

In Response to Religious Pressures

Subtle changes to the language around adoption became obvious after the number of newborn babies available in North America fell to a very low rate. Access to abortions, effective birth control, and women choosing to keep their babies reduced the number to well below adoptive parents' requests. The language used with the birth mother in many Christian organizations changed from blaming her for a fall from grace to supporting her courage in placing her child for adoption. Adoption became a selfless, loving act for a wise birth mother. The implication was that if she kept her baby, she was selfish and immature.

In the early 2000s, evangelical groups began to advocate for a Christian mission to rescue orphans by adoption. They cited scripture to support the notion that Christians were called to bring orphans into their homes as a way of both advancing the role of Christianity in the world and ensuring their own salvation. The movement gained momentum, with congregations bringing in increasing numbers of orphans, usually from other countries and usually of another race. Some adoptive parents were grateful for the addition to their family and truly had wanted to adopt. Others paraded their mixed-race children as proof of their Christian faith. The process became complicated. If God willed that a family must adopt, then any obstacles to that adoption—laws, agency oversight, the best interests of the adoptee, and consideration for birth parents —were against God's will. It became easy for faith-based adoption agencies to ignore anything that stood in the way of their supply of children. The needs of birth families were disregarded. [7]

There was also a subtle motive of reconstruction and assimilation. By adopting children of a different race and incorporating them into their family, these parents could aid in changing the complexion of society. This did not mean that they would preserve the child's culture, affiliation with their birth family, or encourage ties to his or her family or home land. They were to be assimilated into white (for the most part) society in much the same way that Native children were adopted into white families as part of the assimilation of the Indigenous people of America in the Sixties Scoop.

The evangelical Christians' enthusiastic global search for children to adopt and rescue, giving them a "better" life in America, did not examine how life could be improved for the children in their own families and in their own country. A fraction of the money spent on adopting those children could have been used to support them in their own homes. That did not seem to be considered. The notion of "rescue" was the motivator here. Such organizations assumed the home of the North American, Christian rescuer was superior to that of the birth family.

While this was the underlying philosophy of the Orphan Crisis Movement, it was not necessarily the motive of all adoptive parents. We adoptive parents can be part of a greater picture we don't even see. All we see is the child's need for a home and our need for a child. Adoptive parents participated in the adoption of children from Guatemala, Ethiopia, Uganda, Korea, Vietnam, China, Russia, and Haiti without any idea that there might be corruption or moral ambiguity in the process.

To Legalize a Surrogate Birth

Some adoptive parents want to have control over the genetics of their child. Surrogate pregnancies and adoption have a complicated relationship. In these cases, the adoptive parents want the child to either be genetically linked to them or to supervise the pregnancy, or both. Some couples freeze eggs or sperm when they are in their early twenties so that they may be able to use them at a later time in their lives when they are less fertile. Some use eggs or sperm from relatives, some from strangers. The surrogate mother may be artificially inseminated with the father's sperm, which joins with her egg. Another type of fertilization involves the adoptive father's sperm and the mother's egg, which is implanted in the surrogate mother. The baby is genetically the child of the new parents; the surrogate mother carries their child. The generosity of surrogate mothers astounds me—what a gift these women are giving to others.

This is a choice for some, and in Canada it is fairly affordable because health care costs are not factored in. It sounds advantageous, but it creates problems. Because surrogate mothers cannot be paid in Canada, finding one is not easy. In the US, where they can be paid, the cost of hiring a surrogate mother can range between $80,000 and $120,000. Once the child is born, parents must still adopt the child to gain legal custody or they must apply to the courts for a Declaration of Parentage or similar decree because the child is the legal child of the birth mother. There are no standard regulations throughout the country either in Canada[8] or the US.[9] This is a changing field. In Britain, scientists are experimenting with using the DNA of three people to create a child. Many kinds of arrangements are possible and in development in this world of modern and surprising science.

To Create a Loving Environment

Motives for adoption can be obvious or hidden. Usually, by the time we have filled in the adoption forms and met with social workers, adoptive parents are aware of our own motivations. If we have to tell six social workers why we want to adopt, we either understand our motives or we have been telling the same story so often we accept it as real. Sometimes our strongest motive, "I want someone to love," although honest, sounds pathetic, so we find another motive that we think others, specifically social workers, will accept.

Love, while hugely motivating, is not necessarily rational, and North Americans are determinedly rational. Trying to explain the motivating power of love using reason while filling out adoption forms, for instance, is like trying to explain the smell of roses using the sense of touch. It doesn't compute. And we, as a society, don't seem to accept love as sufficient motivation, and try to justify ourselves by reaching for intellectual explanations.

Wanting someone to love who will love us in return seems a reasonable motive to me, but it may seem too self-serving to blurt out; it isn't our only motive. Many adoptive parents are humanitarian, loving, and altruistic. They are willing to face the challenges of raising an adopted child. They understand they need to tell their child as much as they can about his or her adoption history and avoid the secrecy of the past. They know there will be challenges, but there will be joy and pleasure too in watching that child grow and in helping their son or daughter to thrive in the world.

1   John M. Simmons, "Biological and Adoptive Parenting: The Motives Are the Same, Even as They Change." Huffpost Parents, Huffington Post, September 9, 2013. http://www.huffingtonpost.com/john-m-simmons/biological-and-adoptive-parenting_b_3757253.html

2   Caroline Myss, *Anatomy of the Spirit: The Seven Stages of Power and Healing* (New York: Three Rivers Press, 1996).

3   Robert D. Putman, *Bowling Alone: The Collapse and Revival of American Community* (New York: Simon & Schuster, 2000).

4   John M. Simmons, "Biological and Adoptive Parenting."

5   Ibid.

6   Jesus Palacios Brodzinsky. *Psychological Issues in Adoption: Research and Practice* (Santa Barbara: Praeger Publishers, 2005).

7   Kathryn Joyce, "The Problem With the Christian Adoption Movement," *Huffington Post*, April 2, 2013. http://huffingtonpost.com/kathryn-joyce/christian-adoption-movement-problems_b_3367223.html

8   Nancy Lam, "Getting Your Name on the Birth Certificate after a Surrogacy Birth," *Oh Baby*, July 17, 2015. http://ohbabymagazine.com/prenatal/getting-your-name-on-the-birth-certificate-after-a-surrogacy-birth/

9   Jacqueline Nelson, "Weak Fertility Laws Put Potential Parents on Shaky Ground," *The Globe and Mail*, February 10, 2015. http://theglobeandmail.com/life/health-and-fitness/health/weak-fertility-laws-put-potential-parents-on-shaky-ground/article22892551/

3 Becoming a Family

There is a certain naïveté that accompanies new parents—both biological and adoptive. We really do think we can avoid all the mistakes of our own parents and craft a unique, loving, calm, uncomplicated family. *We* are going to get it right. It's not likely. We may be different, but we won't be perfect. We will lose our temper, forget to watch our language, miss signs of distress in our children, respond inappropriately to challenges, and commit the errors of parenting that we were sure we would avoid. Like most families, we will blunder along, trying hard, working at getting better, and loving our kids. Luckily, kids are usually forgiving.

I am sometimes amazed at that firm confidence I had when my children were young. I thought I could handle anything they brought up, anything they challenged me with, and I could keep the family strongly knitted together. I lost track of the fact that we were six independent people who had individual ideas. The children had their sibling quarrels, my husband walked away, and the children grew up and took jobs in different cities. This is all fairly common and many people experience this—after all, the divorce rate is high,[1] and the job market is global, but somehow, when the children were small, those possibilities didn't enter my head. Perhaps we can only plan for the years up to the teens, and then we have to let go and allow our nearly adult children to find their own paths. We do have a great deal of control over the family when the children are little, and it is wise to give them our time and effort then so that we can reap the benefits when they are older. That much seems possible, and that much was possible for me. After the teen years, the kids made their own decisions. They love me, but they started their own families and created their own places to belong, and they rarely discuss with me their feelings about adoption.

Things have changed since my children were teens. New information on what adopted children think and feel allows adoptive parents to anticipate their children's needs more accurately than we could in the past. Adoptive parents have more reason for confidence now.

Expectations

A new member of a family naturally impacts everyone in that family. Some families plan the addition for years, and the new member slides into the space ready for him or her to the satisfaction of the rest. Some adoptees drop into the new family environment with little preparation on either side. The adoption process usually takes months if not years, so precipitous delivery is not the usual method. But even when the arrival of the new child, whether a baby or a teenager, is anticipated, reactions will occur, both expected and unexpected.

Adoptive parents may have a vision of their future. The baby will sleep in his animal-theme bedroom and be praised by all the relatives. The toddler will sing nursery songs with other little children at the library story hour, and we, mother or father, will beam with pride. The older child will love playing baseball with Dad and cooking with Mom, or vice versa. We have visions of sharing our lives with our children, of creating a safe and happy environment where they can grow into their potential. We know that these are only moments in a life that will be filled with the work, struggles, joys, and challenges of children, but we have faith that we can make it happen.

We might do just that. Other people have, so the chances are good we can as well. The enthusiasm and goodwill radiating from those "pick-me" websites where prospective parents offer their profiles are inspiring. So much love and good intentions really do count in making the adoption process work for the parents and the child.

Expectations for continuity and permanence

My sons' birth certificates state they were born to me and my husband. This is a great relief, legally. No one can deny them access to their rights as a child of mine or to their right to inherit and share equally in the family assets. That's good—but "as if born to" is a little skewed, in fact, very skewed.

Children need to know they were born as the child of a particular person. One teen told me, "I feel like I was dropped from an alien ship. No parents. No connections."[2] This is the flip side of "as if born to." It is, on the one hand, positive that children have equal rights in the family but, on the other, it is difficult for them to truly feel as if their life started when they were adopted—because it didn't.

In the past, families went to great lengths to deny or hide adoption, so that the child didn't know they were born to someone else. Secrecy rarely succeeded as there was always some aunt operating under a bit too much wine who let the secret out or someone who felt it was his or her duty to inform the child. In any case, children usually find out. In the evolving world of adoption theory, we need to work out what is the best way to assure adoptees have a firm and legal place in our family while, at the same time, accepting they still have a place in another.

Expectation that differences of race will be accepted by society

If we are accepting of different races ourselves, we may not be aware of the prejudice of others and how that might affect our family. When I adopted my sons, I was colour-blind, and it did not serve me well. Because I thought all races were acceptable and normal, I was not prepared for the racism and bias that surfaced for my youngest son. Because I wasn't prepared, I didn't prepare him very well. He had to sort through it without the kind of education and support I might have provided if I hadn't been so naïve.

I was not prepared for what happened when walking with my adult son and three little grandchildren in downtown Edmonton, Alberta, last year. We were searching for a restroom for the kids, and I suggested we go into a nearby luxury hotel.

"They'll have a restroom there, near the restaurant."

"*You* can go in there, Mom, but I can't, and I'm not taking the kids in there to be insulted. We'll use the library. It's close by."

I realized that my son was right. I was white and therefore acceptable in a luxury hotel. He was Native and might be asked to leave.

"It's downtown Edmonton, Mom. They don't know me from the addicts on the street." There are white addicts on the street too, but I would be able to walk into the hotel without being mistaken for one. My heart just bled; I had truly not prepared him for this.

Fears

Fear we will never have a child

One of our first fears is that we will never find a child at all: we won't be chosen by the birth mother; we won't be allowed to adopt by the laws of our state or province; or our application will be ignored.

I remember phoning the social worker and asking why my

friend received her adopted child and I hadn't—as if there was a list of virtuous and deserving adoptive parents, and I wasn't on it. Social workers seemed to hold the power to provide the baby, and I did not see any particular criteria for who the lucky parents were and who had to wait. Where in past years social workers chose the family, today more birth mothers pick adoptive parents. I couldn't bear to see others matched with a baby while I still waited. I imagined I would learn that it was out of my control, that I was powerless and would simply have to accept the wait.

The fear that you may never get a baby is common to adoptive parents. Some parents do wait for years, so the fear is rational. I waited only nine months for my first son and a year for my second. That would be considered almost instant now. Today, adoptive parents search, fill in forms, create profiles, figure out how to put a video online, even advertise, and still may have to wait for years. More counselling is available today than in the past, so adoptive parents may be more realistic about the time it takes to find the child and thus more patient with the process. I would have been howling in frustration if I had had to wait the four or five years that is common today. It takes maturity and patience to reconcile to the waiting period. Luckily, there are support groups and other expectant adoptive parents who are going through the same process who can help.

Fear we will not pass inspection

Adoptive parents may be afraid they won't pass all those inspections, clearances, and home studies. The list for clearances in many jurisdictions includes a criminal background check, criminal history affidavit, child abuse registry check, medical reports, psychiatric evaluation or a report from a psychiatrist (if you have one), business references, recent tax information, and birth, marriage, and divorce certificates. This is when you worry that that driving-while-under-the-influence charge you got eighteen years ago will damage your chances.

As much effort goes into a home study as you might put into a PhD thesis. Canada Adopts!, an open adoption profile service, advises, "At first glance the requirements for a home study can seem extensive and daunting."[3] It seems daunting at second and third glances, as well. The study can take from three months to a year and asks for information about all aspects of your life. It is important to give as much information as possible so the social worker can assess any hidden tendencies to homicidal mania or social pathology, but it can be exhausting to complete all the information required.

In Ontario, Canada, as in many other places, parents are required to take a course on parenting (at an average cost of $1,400).[4] I am sure I would have benefitted from such a course. The parenting course, a prerequisite before adoption, is meant to provide a thoughtful and deliberate process that prepares them to be parents, as much as it is possible to be prepared for such a complex future. Since several interviews with the social worker are usually part of the home study, two in some states and provinces and three or more in others, adoptive parents must develop a facility for talking about their feelings, something that is not always easy. Social workers will want your views on "marriage, family, income, health, and parenting."[5] But "relax," they advise, and "be yourself." I imagine that is difficult, perhaps impossible, when the outcome of the interview is so important.

Among the suggestions on the Adoption Options website about what to do while you are waiting is to take a CPR course or a parenting workshop—or that vacation that won't be possible with a new baby. I took my two older kids up the Alaska Highway on a six-week summer trip while we were awaiting our youngest child. We did have a friend ready to take *the* phone call from the social worker should a baby become available. We checked in with our friend every few days as we roamed the north with a suitcase full of baby clothes. Our youngest arrived immediately after we returned.

Since waiting for a child can take a long time, planned activities that increase your parenting education and abilities or contribute to your total well-being make sense and may help to ease the overwhelming feeling of powerlessness you might have in this situation.

Fear the birth mother will change her mind

Adoptive parents fear that the birth mother (or father) will place the child and then demand it back. I remember the bone-shaking fear that this would happen to me.

The case of Baby Jessica[6] in Michigan is a grim reminder of birth parents' rights. While the fear that someone will take your baby may seem irrational to an outsider, adoptive parents know how strong their love for their child is and can imagine that a birth mother might have that same strong love and therefore the motivation for trying to reclaim the child. I never thought that a birth father might have that same strong need for a child, but in the case of Baby Jessica, the birth father had not been consulted about the adoption and wanted it stopped. Birth fathers who have not been consulted about adoption (called legal-risk adoptions) and whose rights have not been extinguished can claim the child.[7] Depending on the state or province, the father may have a year to register this claim. In the case of Baby Jessica, the father registered his claim within five days of the baby's birth, and the adoptive parents battled for two-and-a-half years before losing the child.

The possibility of the birth mother or father snatching the child back is every adoptive parent's fear. The fact that it rarely happens (less than one percent of the time)[8] doesn't mean that it can't happen, and this can give us anxiety attacks. The birth mother seems to wield tremendous power.

This may be behind some parents' need for a closed adoption or an international adoption where the birth parents are far removed from the adoptive family. However, open adoption serves the child best and it behooves us, as adoptive parents, to ramp up our courage and deal with the birth parents. A good lawyer will ensure that the correct procedures are followed and you and your child don't end up in a legal mess.

At the time I adopted my children, adoption was usually finalized when the child was one year old. My younger son was three when his adoption was completed. While there was no approach from his birth mother during this time, I breathed a sigh of relief that it would now take a court order to pull him from my arms, rather than simply a decision by a social worker.

Birth mothers sometimes work with the adoptive parents during pregnancy and then change their minds and keep the baby after the birth. This is a huge disappointment to adoptive parents. It doesn't happen often, but often enough that adoptive parents realistically fear it and usually are counselled to prepare for it.

Fear we will not bond

Some adoptive parents fear they will not bond with the child, that they will be mismatched, that bonding will never occur, and everyone will be unhappy.

Some adoptive mothers (and fathers, too) are stunned when, at the first meeting at the hospital, the social worker's office, or the airport, they don't form an instant bond. This need seemed unreasonable to me, although it does happen; there *is* such a thing as love at first sight. My eldest son tells me that he bonded instantly at his son's birth, but it seems reasonable that most of us take a little more time. It is easier, I believe, for an adoptive mother who is also a biological mother to accept this and to consider that taking time to bond is normal. My first child was biological and in hospital with me for three weeks after her birth. It was a time of crisis and drama, and I had little time to relax with her. We got on with our bonding when we went home, and we have a very strong tie to this day. My second child was adopted and had to fit into the family. It seemed to take about six months before he decided that I was worth bonding with and we quickly moved into the glued-together stage. My youngest child came to us at eleven days old and bounced straight into our hearts. I didn't ever consider that bonding might never occur. Of course it would happen; it just might take time. I assumed if I loved my children and was sensitive to them, they would love me back. As a public health nurse, I knew bonding did eventually happen, perhaps to a greater or lesser extent, but certainly it happened.

The adoptive mother may believe she is more enthusiastic than her partner and worry that the partner will not bond with the child. Adoptive parents may worry that the grandparents will not accept the child, particularly if he or she is of a different race. Yes, they may have talked about this with the social worker, but when the social worker holds the child they want, parents may feel reluctant to express any negative feelings and will minimize potential reactions from racially prejudiced relatives.

Bonding can occur despite the attachment disorders that may be present in adopted children who have varying levels of reaction to separation from their birth mother. A child can be truly bonded to his adoptive parents while still reacting to that primary separation. Adoptive parents aren't in a competition with the birth mothers. A child who has been separated from his biological mother through, for example, an extended hospitalization, can also experience separation anxiety and concerns about being abandoned while still maintaining a strong bond with his parents. One doesn't exclude the other.

Today's adoptive parents are usually well aware of the necessity of dealing with the child's trauma of separation from the birth mother. What I considered personality traits in my children, today's psychologists would likely label as some degree of birth-trauma reaction. Children are idiosyncratic and differ in their reactions to separation from the birth mother. Adoptive parents are now usually educated about this issue and can be alert to reactions and be ready to reassure and listen.

Fear that birth family will interfere

Adoptive parents may fear that, in an open adoption, the birth mother will interfere in the family. While open adoption and informal agreements around visiting and contact can work very well, some families—both birth and adoptive families—want a more formal contractual agreement. This can reassure adoptive parents that the birth family will not want to co-parent. Open adoption does not mean co-parenting. Experience shows that rather than interfering in the raising of the child, most birth mothers drift away and it is the adoptive mother who pushes for contact.[9] While the ideal open adoption involves the birth family and adoptive family united in the child's best interests, planned arrangements aren't always fulfilled. It pays to keep in mind that you can manage what comes up; your child will be bonded like Velcro to you; you will make decisions that will further your child's happiness; others have experienced successful open adoptions, and you can as well. Your placement agency can give you good advice here and dispel some of your fears.

Fear of inappropriate contact with birth family

Adoptive parents fear that social media will allow their child to have a hidden relationship with his or her birth mother, that the birth mother or a member of the birth mother's or father's family will contact their child and develop a relationship outside the adoptive parent's supervision.

Open adoption and good communication with the birth parents is most often in the child's best interests, but that communication needs to occur within the boundaries and with safeguards that promote the child's welfare. It is almost impossible for adoptive parents to regulate social media with tech-savvy kids, even those as young as eight. They know how to use Facebook, email, Pinterest, and Instagram on their smart phone. If adoptive parents try to control their children's devices, they'll use their friends' smart phones or computers in the local library. It is the task of adoptive parents to talk to their child about the kinds of communications that are healthy and supportive and the kinds that are disturbing. By the time the children are old enough to engage in social media, they should be accustomed to discussing their feelings with their adoptive parents.

Adoptive parents create contracts or agreements with the birth parents about the kind and frequency of communications with their child and, if the relationship in an open adoption is a good one, this agreement will protect and support the child. However, it may have no influence over members of the birth parents' extended families, and overtures may be made by others, such as siblings. Adoptive and birth parents need to be alert to this. At eighteen, this contact may be very welcome. At eight, it may be confusing and anxiety-inducing. Adoptive parents need to talk about this with their children and prepare for it.

Realities

The real joy of family

You may have decided at the beginning of the adoption process that you wanted to experience that elusive happy family life that seemed to hold so much promise—and now you are. When the child is placed in your family and you begin the work of creating a loving environment, a truly rich emotional life develops. While it takes skill, imagination, and an amazing amount of hard work and money, family life has rewards. The school concerts, the whispered confidences, the serious discussions about childhood problems, the awkwardly constructed Mothers' Day cards, and the sparkling enthusiasm and intense concentration your children focus on you and on their activities can be a constant joy. Even identity crises, the hostility of teen life, the foolish risk-taking and worries of adolescence are deviations, and eventually the child swings back to the solid core of family life. It is, for parents, an incredible experience.

While adoptive parents usually want to remove a child from a difficult family situation and bring her into one in which she will be loved and have more opportunities, they also want to improve their own emotional lives. Children hero-worship you. Really, who else does? Your partner is more realistic, and while he or she might love you, they don't think of you as crowned royalty. Unless you are a celebrity, your children are the only ones who think you are totally wonderful. It's a heady sensation. Even when they become adults and realize that you are not quite as strong, smart, and universally regarded as they once thought, they still think you are wonderful. That's intoxicating.

Children offer us a new world view. They see things differently from us and in ways we might not have considered. My eldest boy seemed to be born with an optimistic view that wonderful things were always going to happen. When he began to experience his share of difficulties—kids like him with attention deficit disorder can have a hard time at school—this attitude astounded me. He was intelligent and imaginative and knew creative ways to drive me crazy. Still, I knew I could count on him to join me in any adventure I planned, because whatever happened, he maintained his eager view that, out there somewhere, was a rainbow.

The expansion of our world

Children often look at the world through a different lens and give you a new perspective. I remember sitting by a pond with my five-year-old youngest son watching the ducks take off and land. He, as a boy who studied airplanes, informed me that these ducks had their flaps and landing gear down. I hadn't considered birds aerodynamically before. He gave me a new way of observing them.

Children are also often good judges of others. My daughter informed me once that a relative was very nice but she only smiled with her teeth, not her eyes. She was quite right; the relative was untrustworthy, and my daughter, at the age of six, knew it.

Dads learn about ballet and become vitally interested in it because their children are up there on the stage. Mothers keep track of hockey-team standings, a subject of absolutely no interest to them until their child started playing. If your child is of another race, you find yourself observing prejudice you had never seen before, and you find a new culture to bring into the family, even a new life philosophy that the culture offers. If you are a writer, you find yourself writing books about that new world.

Our assumptions will be truly challenged

Children can challenge our assumptions with their incessant questioning, "Why?" A feeble response of, "We always do it that way" makes us question our motives. Teens want to know the reasons, in detail, for obeying rules, being socially appropriate, and adhering to laws. They force us to consider who the rules serve and if they are worth preserving. With increasing media focus on entitlement of the rich and a culture of political disdain for the disadvantaged, children who are sensitive to fair dealing may question our apparent acceptance of such a philosophy. As parents we can find ourselves discussing a news broadcast that is filled with racial slurs, acceptance of violence, and elitism, and try to work out with our children our view of a just world. Our children won't let us ignore these influences. They will demand that we grow and mature—one hopes before they do.

We really won't be graded

Emotional richness can be synthesized by the stresses of a family. Our relationship with our partner can and probably will be stressed when a child arrives. Working through the sleep deprivation, worry, and preoccupation with the child can result in a deeper relationship with our partner, and more coping skills. It can create distance as well, but parents, particularly adoptive parents, are aware that this can occur and work to counteract it. When I was a new mother, I experienced something no one had warned me about: It was almost a year before I realized that motherhood wasn't a professional job or a test for which you got a grade. It was a living situation that changed constantly, and I was expected to simply do as well as possible. Apparently, professional women who are mothers often expect themselves to do the "motherhood" job as they did the teaching or engineering job and expect themselves to be competent all the time. It doesn't happen. We muddle through as everyone else does and hope for the best. I was much happier with myself after I accepted that I wouldn't be perfect.

Adjustment to our finances

Usually, adoptive parents have had to prove to social welfare agencies that they have the financial means they need to look after a child. This helps to reduce some of the causes of stress that a child brings to the family. Adoptive parents will have planned for the financial challenges of the child and so are unlikely to blame her or him for the reduction in disposable income. We usually have what we need, but we may have an overinflated idea of the importance of money; we may think that love and money will protect our child from all problems. Perhaps we don't articulate that, but we may harbour the idea that we can cope with most problems because we can afford to. That's true of some problems, but not all. Some families who have to pull together and struggle financially grow closer because they are interdependent. If Mom and Dad are working and the eldest child has to get the meal together, she or he is important to the family. If the maid prepares the meal, the children don't, and parents have to find other ways to create a cohesive family unit.

Having enough money to pay for medical insurance (in the US) and save for education makes life much easier for a family of means, but drug addiction, bullying, challenges to identity, ADD, physical handicaps, diseases, accidents, and psychiatric maelstroms happen in all types of families, including adoptive families. With the exception of paying for medical costs in the US, money won't necessarily solve any of those problems, though it often helps. Adoptive parents usually have worked out how they are going to pay for family expenses well before they become a family.

Experiences of Love

Like most parents, adoptive parents are committed to loving their children. We believe that love can conquer anything. Usually we have a strong bond with our partner and perhaps with our parents and siblings, so we have experience with the glue-like nature of love; it's strong, it sticks, and it's reliable. We bring that to the adoption process. Our kids don't have a chance—we are going to love them. Love gives us a default position upon which to stand when chaos reigns. Whatever else happens, we know we love our children, and we try to do as much as we can to promote their health and safety.

We know love is fundamental but it's not the only thing our children need. Sometimes they need the wisdom of a seer, the listening skills of a psychologist, the diagnostic ability of a doctor, and the educational acumen of a university educator—and they expect all that from us. It's overwhelming at times. Just when we think we've made the best decision possible and given them good advice, we find we've erred and steered them in exactly the wrong direction. This is where love cushions mistakes; forgiveness is part of the loving pattern, and we go on together.

I believe that a healthy family needs love, and intangible as it seems, it's vital. It is hard to describe love, although a vast song-writing and novel-publishing world tries. Both children and adults know love when we have it. Love is not a glorious country where inhabitants live in blissful harmony. It is a messy, shifting, bumpy landscape where parents and children negotiate daily challenges—but behind a rock-solid wall of love. Children may have trouble trusting that it will stay with them and keep expecting love to be withdrawn, but as parents, most of us know we are committed for life to love our children—most of the time.

In all families, relationships occasionally break down. In adopted families, this is called "adoption disruption." It seems odd there is a special name for it. In non-adopted families it might be called "distancing" or "rejection." Whatever it is called, it is experienced as rejection in both adoptive and non-adoptive families. In rare cases, love fails to bind a family. In adoptive families, only two percent break down after all the paperwork has been completed.[10] It is difficult to find statistics for rejection in biological families, but the divorce rate for the US (as of June 2014) was roughly half the marriage rate,[11] so one might assume that household stability in one of two households is fraught for many children. Life can be difficult; relationships are challenging no matter what the constitution of the family, but love does make a difference. For most families love does, indeed, support and sustain relationships.

1   Andrew Feldstein, "Divorces Rate 2013." Feldstein Family Law Group, 2013. http://separation.ca/wp-content/uploads/FELDSTEIN-FAMILY-LAW-Divorce-Fact-Sheet-2013.pdf

2   Marion Crook, *The Face in the Mirror: Teens and Adoption* (Vancouver: Arsenal Pulp Press, 2000.)

3   "Home Study," *Canada Adopts!*, canadaadopts.com/hoping-adopt/home-study/

4   Adopt Ontario PRIDE (Parents Resources of Information Development and Education). https://secure.adoptontario.ca/pride.main.aspx

5   "Home Study," *Canada Adopts!*

6   Gavron Stevens and Darlene and Patricia Tennison, "Adoptive Parents Fear 'Baby Jessica' Legacy," *Chicago Tribune*, July 24, 1993. http://articles.chicagotribune.com/1993-07-24/news/9307240206_1_birth-father-adoptive-parents-cara-clausen.

7   "Adoption Laws," National Adoption Center. [No date]. http://www.adopt.org/adoption-laws

8   Carolyn Berger, "Conquering Birthmother Fear/Vanquishing Birthfather fear. Fact Sheet," *American Fertility Association*. http://www.path2parenthood.org/article/conquering-birthmother-fear-vanquishing-birthfather-fear

9   "Open Adoptions," *Canada Adopts!*, [No date]. canadaadopts.com/
        adopting-in-canada/open-adoption/

10   Stephanie Pappas, "The Dark Side of Adoptions: Why Parents and Kids Don't
        Bond," *Live Science*, April 19, 2010. http://livescience.com/11007-dark-side-
        adoptions-parents-kids-bond.html

11   "Marriage and Divorce," Center for Disease Control and Prevention, November
        21, 2013. http://www.cdc.gov/nchs/fastats/marriage-divorce.htm

4 Successful Parenting

Our Vision

We start our family lives with a positive vision of what our wonderful partner and children will be like, what amazing experiences we will have, and what a joyous home we will create. It's a good thing we begin that way, for we will have to adjust, adapt, and compromise with all the personalities that make up that family to create one that works for us. That early vision can help guide us in the way we want to proceed, but we are going to have to keep rewriting the script to accommodate the needs and particular goals of each member of the family. It's not going to be the perfect family we first envisioned, but if we are sensitive to everyone's needs, we can create one that is stable, supportive, and gives us joy.

When we first think about adoption, many of us believe we can parent very well, or at least better than our own parents. Surely it can't be that hard? We observe the screaming toddler at the restaurant or the rude teen in the corner store, and we know our children will not behave that way. We have studied parenting and know how we can access national associations and local groups of interested people.

In my town, there are many programs for pre-schoolers and teens, including Success by 6, Kids in Motion, speech and language programs and those that support child development, story-time at the library, multicultural groups, drop-in parent and child groups, and directed services for Native children—even some specific to adoptive families. There are online groups for adoptive parents. Where were all these programs when I lived on a ranch, alone all day with pre-schoolers? I could have used some help. Then I was dependent on my creativity and imagination to keep my little ones busy, and I was desperate for knowledge. Now we are spoiled for choice with programs that offer support, knowledge, skills, and that oh-so-important socialization with other parents.

Today's parents can feel the standards of parenthood are impossibly high. They may feel pressured to take every class they can, particularly if they have a long pre-adoption wait. There is so much available, it's confusing. It's like standing in front of the ice cream counter with offerings of chocolate, truffle, maple pecan, caramel pretzel, blood orange, and pistachio lined up and available, and wanting them all—and right now. We do try to learn as much as we can. Then our children arrive with their histories, personality traits, and vulnerabilities, and we wonder how anyone could possibly learn enough to deal with these highly complex children.

What Skills Do We Need?

Ability to maintain humour and optimism

Humour is essential. If we can't laugh at our attempts to parent, then we might as well order a year's supply of lorazepam. Anxiety builds when too much challenge meets too little skill.[1] We feel out of our depth, unprepared, and unsure of our options. Humour dissipates low-level anxiety, but it doesn't work on the over-the-top, paralyzing high anxiety. High-level anxiety may need medical treatment. Oddly, and this seems counter-intuitive, humour can make high-level anxiety worse.[2] But humour works like a drug on the everyday anxiety we feel when we are faced with stress. If we can laugh or even smile, our challenges seem less severe. Chemically, laughter or the sense of the ridiculous releases the happy quartet of dopamine, serotonin, oxytocin, and endorphins in the brain, and we relax.[3] We get relief from tension—even if our challenges remain—without side effects. Those who consciously use humour to lessen anxiety have lower blood pressure than those who don't.[4]

We need all the help we can get to keep our perspective on life positive and our blood pressure low because anxiety and fear of what might happen is common in imaginative, intelligent, and perceptive people, which includes most of the adoptive parents I've met. We think about what might happen to threaten us and our loved ones. Those fears aren't necessarily irrational. When we have children, we fear for them. We are parents; we are never anxiety-free. The trick is to keep humour a constant companion and use it to keep anxiety levels on a comfortable level.

Optimism is the twin of humour. Optimistic people—and surely adoptive parents are optimistic—expect to succeed in creating a loving family. That's one of the reasons we so often succeed. Our optimism about our children conveys our expectations that they will be good people. Most of the time, they turn out to be just that.

Ability to recognize what we don't know

It is a virtue to understand that we don't, as parents, know everything. We may be buoyed up by the euphoria of new parenthood for quite some time before we realize that this child didn't come with an instruction manual and we are at a loss. Parents who have biological children share some of these feelings. As a friend of mine complained, "They come out of the egg so different."

But adoptive parents cope with the usual challenges, plus some differences. And there are differences. While we are committed to this child as if she was born to us, she wasn't, so we need to check out how that fundamental difference is going to affect our child and our family. I have a step-daughter, a biological daughter, and two adopted sons. I had to try to understand what differences were attributable to adoption vs. biology, male vs. female roles, and birth order. Recently I found that birth order has little significance,[5] but it was a theory that influenced many when my children were small, and I considered it. Expectations for one child can't be applied to another. As parents we are constantly noticing those differences.

Ability to embrace realistic expectations

Our expectations as parents are a balance between what we know of child development in general and the knowledge of our child's particular concerns, obstacles to development, fears, and strengths. One eight-year-old can be left to knock on doors on your block and sell Scout troop cookies while another would fear abduction and couldn't do it without an adult. They are different and we need to work out what they need and what we can realistically expect of them. It's not easy.

My eldest son was lively, impulsive, and full of laughter and loud conversation. It took some time for me to accept that his personality and character were programmed at birth and while I could help him make decisions, I couldn't and shouldn't change him. I would be better off to accept his kinaesthetic way of learning (trying everything once). Having come to this point following much introspection and study, it astounded me when, after caring for him for a few days, my mother commented dryly, "It's nice to see you getting your own back." Apparently, I was much like him as a child. Who knew?

The world gets more and more complicated as well. What we experienced as children is not what our children experience.

They seem to have so many more decisions to make that require a sophistication we didn't achieve until adulthood. Many parents today try to keep toy guns out of their homes. That seemed odd to me until I realized that guns were used to hunt when I was a child and when I raised children in a rural area. Now, guns are associated with gangs and crime, and the notion that guns are toys seems fraught with symbolism. Parents fear their children will consider gangs and crime normal. It's a problem—it's unreasonable to have a philosophical discussion about the symbolism of guns with a six-year-old.

Parents also have to make decisions about the surveillance and supervision of their children. How much is important for their safety and how little is necessary for the development of independence? It is tempting to keep children close to us for all time. As parents, we feel we can keep them safer than they can themselves, and for a very long time this is true. But letting them find their confidence to be independent is important, and it is one of the most difficult skills of parenting. Children achieve independence in a patchy manner. Your sixteen-year-old can ask you to find his socks and at the same time ask for the car keys. With that kind of patchy development of independence, it is very hard to know when to hold the child close and when to step back.

There are no universal guidelines on how to create sturdy independence in your child. Some living situations are much more dangerous than others. Some dangers your child can manage—stay off thin ice, tie your horse when you dismount or you will be walking home, lock up your bike, keep your cell phone charged, and come straight home from school. And there are others that you must manage—choosing which homes are safe for a sleepover, which school district is likely to give a safe environment, which neighbourhood to settle in, which relatives are safe for your child to spend time with, particularly if your child is a different race from you, and whether it is safe to walk to school. The parents and the child need to work out how independence happens. Social situations, living conditions, and the child's ability to plan and use judgement are all factors parents weigh. And they do it all the time, every day.

Ability to seek experience and advice

It seems as though we never have enough experience to face the challenges children bring us. The minute we think we know what we're doing, the child does something that flummoxes us. It may be, as my aunt told me, children are sent to keep us humble. They certainly manage to do that.

It helps to be informed about the ages and stages of child development so we can be ready to adjust and prepare our children for the difficulties of the coming stage, but I guarantee they'll come up with something that isn't in any book and no one has ever considered before. A doctor friend told me once that accomplished, professional parents had a hard time being parents because they thought they should be able to be perfect at it, and parenthood doesn't allow perfection. There isn't a child-raising manual tucked into the baby blanket that guarantees results.

If we are lucky, we have our own parents as good mentors who can give us the benefit of their experience. In today's world, those parents may be working full time, live a thousand miles away, or be estranged. My parents lived 400 miles away and were estranged from me when I was raising my children. Fortunately, I had a neighbour who was wise and gave me advice when I asked. She was the principal of an elementary school and had seen a wide range of behaviours in kids. She had an amazing sense of humour and a practical approach to children. As I had to forge my own way through the parenthood maze, it was wonderful to have her advice on a few shortcuts. Look for teenagers you admire and get friendly with their parents. Advice can be useful.

There is an inexhaustible supply of advice online. Some of it is professional, some from experienced adoptive parents, some in the form of a blog as parents try to figure out the parenting process. There are lists of recommended sites and reading materials, both online and in real in-your-hand books. For Canadians, the Dave Thomas Foundation[6] has a long list and, for Americans, Adoption Online[7] has a site categorized by subject that will take you to lists of reference material. It all helps, but face-to-face discussion with an adoption professional is exceptionally valuable.

In some areas of both Canada and the US, parent groups meet regularly for discussion and education. In many towns and cities, psychologists educated in adoption issues can shore us up and steer us in the right direction. While I'm not sure there is a "village" available to help raise a child, there is certainly the possibility of a team. We can create this team of professionals, fellow adoptive parents, extended family, and best friends. Knowing when to ask for help is important. Knowing where to get the *best* help is a developed skill. Attending groups and listening to the experience of others can be vastly helpful in directing us toward preferred professionals.

Cheaper than professionals (free) and usually available is the advice of a mother, mother-in-law, aunt, or anyone whom we trust to be a good mentor. They are often available at the end of the phone. Not all are useful, but some are. A best friend whose children are a little older than ours or who raised adoptees can be heaven-sent. There ought to be organizations around the country comprised of people who have experience with the problems we face and who are willing to act as mentors. We could all benefit from someone who knows what it's like. When we are stressed or overwhelmed, we could call on our mentor to drop everything and come over. I fantasize about a psychologist in my back pocket whom I could pull out, set on the table, and tell my troubles to. I'd get objective, educated, and informed advice. Sometimes desperation impels us to seek advice from anyone who will listen. Ah well. My mother, who had six kids, used to go once a week to the hairdresser's—her substitute psychologist. I expect the hairdresser knew more about our family than we did.

Ability to problem-solve

Most of us reach adulthood with some ability to problem-solve. What we may not be ready for is the finely honed skill of problem-solving four or five challenges at once—and at high speed. It's one of those "in the trenches" skills that improve with practice. You'd think that nurses would have an edge on this skill because we are often forced to problem-solve under pressure and with multiple problems, but, somehow, it's different when we are reacting to our own family members. For one thing, the basic respect we usually get from patients may be absent for the moment in our family, and for another, we have more emotional investment in the outcome when it's *our* kid who thinks he is going to stay out all night. Riding our own emotions while problem-solving is a challenge.

Ability to accept differences

Some parents deny there is any difference between adopted and biological children. This attitude prevents exploration of possible differences and creates problems in the future. I agree there is no difference in our ability to love our adopted children or for them to love us, but there *are* differences in how they live in the world.

One difference is their ability to get information about themselves. Generations of adoptees can tell you that they needed information and support that parents couldn't give because they pretended the child had been born to them. Facing these differences early can make them much less influential in the child's life. Acceptance of birth families can help reduce the concerns of adoptive parents and contribute to a more secure sense of belonging in adoptees. Adoptive parents are often less threatened by a real birth family than by an imaginary one. Still, not all open adoptions result in a warm and friendly extended family. Life is messy. Families are unpredictable. We do the best we can. But adoptees have a huge need to know about their birth families,[8] and parents who recognize and acknowledge the facts of adoption—and the differences that result—can help their child immensely.

Ability to acquire training and education

There are centres for adoption education in many towns and cities. Adoptive families' associations usually have an education component. Most parents had to take classes when they were planning to adopt and participated in education workshops. The heightened tension parents may have been feeling at that time may not have been the best atmosphere for learning. Prospective parents were aware that the educator and the social agency were assessing them; this caused its own anxiety. Parents were anxious to learn all they could about the particular child they were getting and not necessarily interested in children in general. They were less interested in the tantrums of a two-year-old, for instance, if they were expecting a newborn, and barely listened to explanations and advice. The tantrums of a two-year-old are hugely motivating when they are happening in our house.

Many organizations offer online courses, some free and some

for a price. We can register and take them at home. Some are interactive so we can ask questions and get an answer from the experts. Over time, with a few courses and more experience, we become more knowledgeable. When we have an urgent problem, we often want specific and practical advice. Online courses may not give us that. I have taken a few of them and they are informative, but I get more from an in-person class. If I had a need for specific information, I'd be more inclined to find myself a psychologist who specialized in adoption issues, and if I couldn't find that professional, then I'd look for one who specialized in parenting. General parenting advice that is not specific to adoptees can miss the mark and leave us working hard at trying to help our child without a clear understanding of her difficulties. Professionals who are educated in adoption issues can be far more useful.

And, of course, we read all we can and try to absorb new research and new approaches.

Ability to avoid blaming, reframing, rescuing, and rejecting

There are plenty of maladaptive ways of parenting. All parents have probably slipped into these. Sometimes, we try anything.

Blame is one of the ways we try to make the problems go away. I remember screaming at my two-year-old son, then stopping cold and thinking, "Who is this monster mother? I'm scaring him. I swore I'd never do it. I need to get some help." I went to the mental health clinic in our small town and asked for parenting classes. There weren't any.

"We need some, though," admitted the administrator. "We'll set them up at the high school in the evening for parents, and you can teach them."

I was a public health nurse and took child development courses in university, but I was no expert. Researching for this session of

Have a solid financial plan

The cost of an adoption can be estimated before you start the adoption process. There should be no surprises there. After the adoption is completed and paid for, there is a mountain of expenses. The cost of raising a child in Canada to age eighteen was estimated in 2011 to be $243,660.[9] When you consider daycare costs (and neither Canada with the exception of Quebec, nor the US have universally affordable daycare), this can be much higher. The cost of raising a child in the US was estimated to be closer to $900,000 in 2012, according to an article in *Forbes*.[10] These figures might make a few parents pause and reconsider parenthood. The estimates vary because some include loss of wages from the stay-at-home parent, loss of investment opportunity, and increased housing and sustenance costs. However you calculate it, children do cost a great deal of money, and parents need to plan for that and for the unexpected medical expenses in the US, and orthodontic costs in both countries, as well as the many expenses that we assume for our child such as music and dance lessons, sports camps, psychologist sessions, and vacations. Without the child-centred programs of the Scandinavian countries where child care, long maternity leaves, free education (including university), and universal health care make having children much more affordable, we must plan to set aside this money to support our children. Reading a detailed analysis of child-rearing expenses is enough to make a prospective adoptive parent shiver. We know that it will be worth it, but it is daunting to see the dollars stacked up for years. It's another of those let's-face-the-music moments when we realize that, indeed, we must plan and we must commit. We may have to forego that trip to Paris until the kids are teens—or maybe it will be in our retirement plan.

parenting classes was instructive, and so were the other parents. Somehow we muddled through the theories ("active listening" was in vogue then) and discussed their application, and I stopped yelling—most of the time.

Blaming the child for his or her behaviour isn't always unreasonable. After all, he did take the plate of brownies from the fridge and ate every one. But the danger lies at stopping there. We need to look at why he is behaving the way he does and help him search for better judgement and coping strategies. It's difficult to avoid prolonging the tug-of-war pattern we get into in the toddler stage when the child is often determined to walk into traffic, jump off cliffs, and generally put himself in dangerous situations. We become responsibly hyper-vigilant, but may forget to ease back and let the child take more and more responsibility as he matures. Instead of letting the situation teach the child—if you spend your allowance on one toy, there is no money left over for the movie—we blame the child for his earlier bad decision. It's a habit and can result in keeping the child at a distance as he learns to expect criticism and blame. When children accept blame, they begin to believe they are "bad," at fault, and not good enough for their parents. For adoptees, it is easy to slip into: "I'm not good enough because I'm adopted."

If we don't blame our children, we might try "reframing," the art of altering perspective. Some of the child's concerns may make adoptive parents uncomfortable and so they would like to reframe the concern in order to reduce its importance. Why his birth mother gave him up may not seem crucial to you, since the effect was to send your son into your family, but it can be very important to him. Sometimes reframing is a useful tool in making a huge problem more manageable. Our children may do it themselves if they are given a chance to talk about a problem and view it from different perspectives. But it's tempting to try to make the problem disappear so that we may be more comfortable. Reframing so that a problem is no longer a problem is one way to make it fade temporarily. We can trivialize it by saying it's not important, cajole our child into accepting the situation, or outright deny it happened. If we think it isn't important, we may try reframing it as trivial and assume he will agree with us. Not necessarily. He may simply not talk to us about it anymore and live with anxiety.

We are often also tempted to rescue our child. They do need rescuing when they're young. We aren't going to leave them up that tree or in that tangle of bicycle parts. As they grow, we need to develop the skill of staying in the background while they work out their problems. We all know parents whose thirty-year-old child is living at home because he has never developed the skills to live on his own. I realize that in some areas it is financially impossible, but if this man can't make his own dentist appointment because he never has had to, can't get up on time because Mom always wakes him, can't cook a meal or do laundry, something is wrong. If Mom writes his résumés and gets him job interviews, he'll never be independent. One employer told me that a mother even accompanied her son to his interview.

This may be more likely in small families where parents have more time to oversee each child. I once heard a woman on a radio program in Ireland comment in her musical accent that "The first one you watch every breath. The fifth one you say, 'If you're going to smoke that joint, open the window.'" The more children, the less we worry—perhaps. We may find we can give more attention to our children when we have only one or two. But it may also be true that we perceive more danger for our children than parents did in the past. I was handling a .22 rifle safely off in the woods alone when I was ten years old in our rural area. I wouldn't dream of letting a ten-year-old handle a firearm unsupervised now. Society changes and dangers are different with each generation. Parents try to adjust to this. Allowing your child autonomy without feeding him to the wolves of danger and irreversible harm is a trick in today's world of gangs and random violence. How do we assure they are safe without paralyzing them with our fears? One strategy is to listen and to talk with them about what they can expect and how they can cope.

Parenthood can be so overwhelming that some give up and reject the child. Parents who were motivated when they adopted a child but who eventually coped with the stresses by rejecting the child join the ranks of biological parents who withdraw from their relationship with their child and, in effect, abandon them. Sometimes the rejection of the child happens early, as in the notorious case of Torry Hansen, who put a seven-year-old she had agreed to adopt on the plane back to Russia.[11] This is rare. Most parents battle through the initial difficult stage believing that they can overcome a rough beginning; after all, most children are challenging in some areas. You may look with envy at the sweet, well-behaved child in the grocery store while yours is having a temper tantrum in the cereal aisle, but she is your child (sigh) and you will work with her until she becomes calm. For all you know, that sweet child in the cereal section screams all night. Exchanging stories with other adoptive parents can make our own families seem more normal—and the future seem more possible.

We can focus on the positive experiences with our children to counteract some of the unexpected and unwanted messes we get into with them. They do love their birthday present and thank you enthusiastically; they do help around the house at times; they do laugh and enjoy us and the family. It's just that we often concentrate on what is not working instead of what is.

Ability to cultivate patience

All parents need patience. We can get to the point of feeling over-whelmed, highly anxious, and out of control. We feel we need to stop the world and get off for a moment. It seems that adoptive parents need an extra dollop of patience because we sometimes have to deal with reactions in our child that seem unprovoked. We don't expect these reactions and find ourselves responding to them as if they were the concerns of a strange child. Where did he come from? Adoptees can react to trauma that occurred early in their lives, which we may know little about. Sometimes we don't understand the depth of their feelings but we know that we must drive thirty miles back to the motel to get our son's forgotten "blankie," which we can clearly see in our mind's eye lying abandoned on the motel bed. The operative word may be "abandoned." We aren't sure of anything but that our son will not feel secure if we don't get it back. We may never understand why, and our child might not either. Rightly or wrongly, we can feel it's unfair that our child is throwing those hyper-reactions at us.

Being patient may be especially difficult for parents who have had a career where we were sure of our place in the workforce, knew what to do, and were successful. As parents, we often don't know what to do, and can react to our children as if they were unreasonable and unfair employers. We can resent these strange challenges.

We can also get into the habit of reacting with anger. It may seem to us we have to get angry before our children conform. The escalation to anger can become our default position. We need an objective perspective. Instead of looking at raising children as a long-term war of wills, we can look at it as a long-term teaching project. Our children can teach us patience. Certainly, we need to develop ways of coping so that patience is our default position and anger rarely interferes to prevent us from finding the best solution. Developing patience is an essential learning process for parents. It requires that we be if not comfortable then at least non-reactive when we don't have control of a situation. We need patience to stay with that difficult feeling because we *can't* control every aspect of our child's life.

Learn to Love

Everyone has had some experience of love, however fleeting. We've heard about it, thought about it, and felt it. Can we augment our capacity to love so when troubles hit us like a sudden cyclone, we can ballast our family with our love?

Many of us come to parenthood with habits from our first families that make it difficult for us to develop our ability to love. We may have been told that the hitting, verbal abuse, and beatings we received were done in the name of "love," so we learned to avoid love or withdraw from it. We may have allowed a few trusted people into our world, but our instinctive reaction is to avoid intimacy. Some people experience love as making sacrifices for others and see it as a measure of caring; they feel loved only if surrounded by a needy family. Some have joyous experiences, a past full of adventure and support. We can sort through our own inadequacies and strengths and learn to open ourselves, to become more vulnerable and loving.[12]

For me, love is like music: You know it when you experience it. You enjoy it, luxuriate in it, are enthralled by it, and then it fades and warms your memory. I can reconstruct love in my mind as a pleasurable experience, but I can't feel it until I experience it again. Like music, love can be studied, and many scholarly papers, books, and magazine articles have done so, and their authors speak of different kinds of love.

The notion of a romantic love that is destined for you and sweeps you off your feet is just that, a romantic notion. Much different is enduring love, such as we have for our children. It is practical, reliable, secure, and lasting. And we have to work at it.

Lisa Appignanesi in her book *All About Love: Anatomy of an Unruly Emotion*[13] delineates four types of love based on the work of Aristotle: affectionate; social (friendship); hospitable (charity); and erotic. Appignanesi writes of the love of family and says, "the love parents or carers offer their children radically affects the way they mature—neurally, physiologically, emotionally, mentally." She goes on to explain that although love makes our life worth living, it has a "dark" side that can cause us suffering. Still, without love, we wouldn't know rapture and we wouldn't know ourselves.[14]

We know that. It is one of the reasons we adopted our children. They make our lives richer, more meaningful and purposeful. We offer them support and love, and plough through the tough days in order to bask in the joy of the good ones. That's family.

In spite of the challenges of day-to-day parenting, most adoptive families work through their problems and achieve what the adoptive parents planned—a loving family. The interviews I did with teens on their views of adoption revealed the strong bond they felt with their adoptive parents. That never seemed to be in question. Even when I thought the adoptive parents were less than ideal, the adoptee was still committed to the relationship. They were their parents, and that was that. It's reassuring to know that we don't have to be perfect to be loved.

1   Michael Meany, "Humour, Anxiety, and Csikszentmihalyi's Concept of Flow." http://persons.org.uk/ati/education/cp/ce3/meany%20paper.pdf

2   Ibid.

3   Thai Nguyen, "Hacking Into Your Happy Chemicals: Dopamine, Serotonin, Endorphins and Oxytocin," *Huffington Post*, October 20, 2014. http://huffington-post.com/thai-nguyen/hacking-into-your-happy-c_b_6007660.html

4   Nancy A. Yovetich, T. Alexander Dale, and Mary A. Hudak, "Benefits of Humor in Reduction of Threat-induced Anxiety," *Psychology Reports*, February 1990. http://ncbi.nlm.nih.gov/pubmed/2326429

5   David DiSalvo, "Despite Popular Assumptions, Birth Order Isn't Important, Says New Study," *Forbes*, 2015. http://forbes.com/sites/daviddisalvo/2015/07/20/despite-popular-assumptions-birth-order-isnt-important-says-new-study/

6   "Organizations and Publications: General Adoption Resources." David Thomas Foundation for Adoption Canada. https://davethomasfoundation.ca/about-foster-care-adoption/general-adoption-resources/

7   "Adoption Library," Adoption Online, June 2014. http://adoptiononline.com/adoptionlibrary.html

8   Marion Crook, *The Face in the Mirror: Teens and Adoption* (Vancouver: Arsenal Pulp Press, 2000).

9   Camilla Cornell, "The Real Cost of Raising Kids," *MoneySense*, August 10, 2011. http://moneysense.ca/magazine-archive/the-real-cost-of-raising-kids

10 Jacoba Urist, "American Dream? No Can Do. I'm Too Busy Parenting," *Forbes*, July 12, 2012. http://forbes.com/sites/jacobaurist/2012/07/12/american-dream-no-can-do-im-too-busy-parenting/

11 KJ Del'Antonia, "How to Love an Adopted Child: The Painful Truth about Adoption," *Slate*, April 13 2010. http://slate.com/articles/double_x/doublex/2010/04/i_did_not_love_my_adopted_child.1.html

12 Lisa Firestone, "Making Love Last by Learning to Love," *Psychology Today*, February 1, 2011. http://psychologytoday.com/blog/compassion-matters/201102/making-love-last-learning-love

13 Lisa Appignanesi. *All About Love: Anatomy of an Unruly Emotion* (W.W. Norton & Company: New York, 2011), 273.

14 Ibid., 13.

5 What Children Need and How Parents Can Help

Children have multiple needs: love, attention, care, and appreciation. They have to bond with their parents and family and attain a sense of belonging and affiliation with society, a sense of identity and purpose. They require confidence, curiosity, trust, good health, opportunities, financial security, education, the ability to negotiate social situations, and a way to establish values. It's a wonder we don't quit before we start when we realize we are responsible for this. They also have a need for joy, fun, adventure, and wonder. It's the ability to fulfill these needs and the reciprocity of affection with our children that make parenting worth the tremendous effort.

Special Needs of Adoptees

Adoptees have the same needs as biological children, but they may have additional needs. Early trauma *can* interfere with the physical development of good health and intelligence, although that isn't usual, and our adopted child generally comes to us intelligent and healthy. If they don't, we can identify and work with them and the health-care system to address their problems, which may be challenging and obvious. The emotional effects of early trauma—either the simple fact of being removed from the birth mother, or long-term neglect or abuse—can be hidden and not as obvious. These leave internal scars that interfere with the child's development, and can puzzle and sometimes infuriate parents.

Children's reactions can seem outlandish, inappropriate, and unexpected, as if we had innocently poked a bear. We don't understand their behaviour; we know they are affected by something, but we don't know what it is. Their emotional sensitivities seem beyond our common sense. We need more information if we are going to be able to help them.

To feel love and acceptance

We expect to create a loving family. We know what we need to do and plan for it. Adoption agencies demand we plan for it, so by the time the child is finally in our home, we have a clear understanding of what we need to do in the near future. Sometimes that's easy and sometimes it's difficult. A newborn is often receptive and responsive to us. Older children may take more of our time and effort before they find a unique place in the family and we can relax and enjoy them.

Part of the joy of a family is the way we participate in our children's discovery of the world. We can marvel at the fast-growing beans on the windowsill, the magnificence of the stars, and the humour in the latest kids' movie. At the edge of the sea with my granddaughter, we stopped and watched a snake eat a fish. I would not have seen it if she hadn't been with me, looking for wonders. I stood with her, sharing her fascination.

I have watched soccer, rugby, and hockey games not because I am a fan, but because my children were participating. At one music recital where my six-year-old youngest son was performing, his sister, brother, dad, and I sat in the audience. The whole row of us tensed when he reached the ninth bar. Bar nine was his Rubicon. He faltered. We held our breath. He stopped. No one in our row moved a muscle. He started again from the beginning and breezed right through bar nine. We breathed again.

It's not just being there that makes a family; it's the emotional participation that makes life rich. And, of course, it is that emotional sustenance that makes family so valuable to us. We put effort into birthday parties, Christmas, and other holiday festivities and try to make sure our children know we love them. To ensure that our children accept our love, we need to be knowledgeable about the effects of adoption. If we know that a child might be conflicted about celebrating his birthday and might feel an overpowering sadness on that day, we may be more understanding about his reactions and less inclined to be perplexed or hurt. Kids understand when they are loved and when they are not. We can manage that, but our knowledge of the adoptees' special needs is important as well. With love, we can be supportive and helpful some of the time. With love and knowledge we can be supportive and helpful more often.

To deal with abandonment issues

Most pre-adoption counselling now includes a basic description of abandonment issues, attachment difficulties, and bonding. We listen to these and theoretically understand them, but the theories take on new life when our three-year-old is arching her back and screaming. Is this a manifestation of an abandonment issue or simply frustration at being thwarted? When were adoptive parents expected to morph into psychologists? Do we need a psychologist at every stage of our child's life? It would be handy, but not possible or necessary. Our own sense of what our child needs is usually reliable. Most of the time, we can trust this, but we may look for a psychologist when we are stressed, confused, and frustrated, and when that frustration interferes with the way the family interacts. We may consult a psychologist when we can't deduce why we or the child reacts the way we do and can't see a way out of this pattern.[1] The rest of the time, and that's most of the time, we try to figure out what to do by talking to friends, our partner, other adoptive parents, the teacher or day-care worker, or a trusted older person who knows our family. And perhaps we talk to all of them. Children can make even professionals feel totally incompetent.

In spite of our best intentions and efforts, our child may not feel at home in our family. Or they may feel at home and part of the family, while at the same time a little apart from it, like a visiting relative. Parents are usually aware that a child needs a sense of where they came from, but I doubt we can understand the void that seems to increase as the child matures. They begin to realize they have no solid knowledge of their background; it is a giant black hole. An adopted teen once told me she didn't feel quite human. There is a difference between intellectually understanding that a child might wonder about his ancestors and emotionally appreciating that a child feels like an alien. Many parents do understand this and create "birth books" in which photos of the birth family, the newborn, and the arrival at the adoptive home are used to show the child his or her connections to the past. An open adoption and connection with the birth mother and her family and, if possible, the birth father and his family can give the child that sense of a past. Closed or international adoptions, in which the birth family is unavailable or the history is scanty or inaccurate, make it much more difficult for adoptive parents to provide those connections; these seem to become more important as the child goes through the teen years.

Not every child who is adopted has severe abandonment issues. When the issues are periodic and mild, we count ourselves lucky. When they are serious, their effects can be debilitating for the child and very hard on the family. One of the difficulties is that abandonment issues are not necessarily obvious when the child is young. They often do not surface until the late teens. This coincides with the time when children habitually do not talk to their parents about problems, when they are trying to lead an independent life, and when they see these intrusive feelings as "weird." They can be ashamed of their feelings and feel disloyal to their adoptive parents. It's often a situation in which frank and honest discussion cannot easily take place.

This can be overwhelming for them. Adoptees may have crushing feelings of loneliness, alienation, and rejection. They may feel that they were not wanted by their birth mother—and for whatever reason, even a loving one, that is true. They were not kept, so de facto, they were not wanted. Teenagers tend to think in black and white, in all-or-nothing terms, and see complex situations, including adoption, as a single rejection issue. This can be a hard fact for them to face.

Karen was eighteen years old, living on her own, and going to school when she told me: "I'm having trouble accepting love ... I know there's something inside me I have to deal with. Because my own [birth] mother couldn't keep me, I thought she didn't love me. I still think she didn't love me. This is why, when somebody tells me they love me or somebody tries to show me they love me, I reject it. I mean like, 'Your own mother gave you up. What was the matter with you?'"[2]

That seems to explain how many adoptees feel. Some can encapsulate it as a long-ago problem and some continue to be affected by it. Having once been abandoned, with the disruption of bonding that entails, they fear being abandoned again. Like Karen, they *know* that loss is part of life, that people may love them and leave them, and that they are probably lovable. But they *feel* unlovable, that there is something inherently wrong with them that will cause abandonment in the future. Every relationship becomes tainted with this fear. Not all adoptees experience this, and some don't seem to feel it at all, but some, like Karen, have a fear of being abandoned set into their psyche from an early age. This exists together with a relief at having been placed in their adoptive home. Adoptees often need to ponder, talk about, and attempt to resolve this uncomfortable juxtaposition of feelings.[3]

Avoidance of feelings around abandonment prevents emotional growth. Refusal to confront those feelings does not make them disappear. Escape mechanisms such as compulsive eating, lying, sexual addiction, and substance abuse only allow time to go by; they don't allow teens to mature. Teens facing conflicts of identity can require a great deal of help.

Feelings around identity and belonging are so strong that many adult adoptees report that their emotional development stopped in their late teens while they worked at trying to deal with their reactions to the deep and overwhelming sense of emptiness. Adoptees may feel they don't fit in their adoptive family. This sense of alienation can be profound, particularly if they are of a different race from their birth parents and the adoption is obvious. They may try escape measures such as drugs to dull the pain and set up a pattern of withdrawal from intimacy based on the belief that they must end any relationship before the other person rejects them. These debilitating feelings can occur in spite of loving adoptive families. This is a scary concept for us as adoptive parents. How can we help our children weather these all too common feelings?

Planning for Abandonment Issues

Perhaps if we were educated to expect abandonment issues to start erupting in our child's life in their late teens, we could prepare him or her for this and set up a method of dealing with these feelings, such as counselling. It could be part of the usual maturity activities such as learning to drive, choosing classes in school, and choosing a career. Teens could see a psychologist to deal with adoption issues, an advisor they could pick ahead of time. A series of counselling sessions could be planned as a normal part of a teen's future. This way, adoption issues could be dealt with during the child's teen years and not become a life sentence of intimacy avoidance and emotional escape.

I did not have this insight when my children were teens. My eldest son decided when he was about twenty to examine his past. He thought about his birth with the help of a therapist, compartmentalized it, and concluded it was a time of sadness. This allowed him to isolate that time as in his past, not in his present. He soon met the woman of his dreams, married young, and was a father of two by the time he was twenty-four. I believe his introspection helped him to become an emotionally mature adult, ready for intimacy, but he maintains that he never had big problems with being adopted in the first place. He considers adoption as an accident of birth. Children differ in their views and reactions to adoption. Because some children require a great deal of help to get to a place of acceptance, it would seem wise for parents to prepare them.

Resilience of Adoptees

Resilience is a normal and basic human quality. We know some children seem to be able to work around problems, regroup, and try again to their advantage or, at least, regroup and try again. Some, though, seem to fold and become fearful; they are sure they can't cope. Qualities that contribute to resilience such as high IQ come with the child. A high IQ gives the child a better ability to see more options than a child with a lower IQ.[4] Adoptive children do not, according to some studies, have lower IQ or lower self-esteem than non-adopted children but exhibit the same capacity to be self-reliant and independent.[5]

Resilience is an "ordinary" human trait; adoptive parents can expect their children to have some resilience—they need only to learn how to encourage it. There doesn't seem to be much difference between the advice given to encourage independence and self-esteem in children and that given to encourage resilience. Resiliency seems to be a result of independence and a belief in one's self-efficacy. Specific advice around resilience is to support children in making and carrying out plans.[6]

We know that our children need to feel we've "got their backs" while we encourage them to make their own decisions. It's a delicate parenting skill. Some children need more help to develop their sense of efficacy and resilience than others, and they need more or less support at different times in their lives. The resulting resilience and feelings of capability that we encourage so strongly have to be tempered with consideration of others and with a vast amount of kindness. I am not advocating that our children be so independent they end up as narcissists. A truly self-efficient, resilient person without the mitigating quality of kindness would make a good gangster.

Establishing Identity within the Family

We establish identity throughout our lives. The toddler who learns "Mama" and "Dada" learns her identity in relation to her family and to concrete objects and locations such as her home. She explores her environment and finds her place in it. She knows where she belongs. She learns where she belongs in her family.

Adoptive parents must be clear about what position each child in the family occupies. Biological children will jockey for position and settle into what works without much direction or consideration from parents. Adopted children may need more direction in order to understand and feel confident of their position.[7] It may feel tenuous to them, as if they were constantly in danger of falling from the family tree. They may continually test their sense of place within the family, striving for a secure hold on their particular branch. We need to remind ourselves that what seems obvious to us may not be obvious to our child and he may need to be told that his position as the youngest (or eldest or middle) child is important.

Pre-teen children establish their identity in concrete terms: as a six-year-old hockey player, an eight-year-old violin player, an achiever at school, a dunce at math, a Boy Scout, a member of a religious group, a good swimmer, or someone who is afraid of the dark. Children name many aspects in their lives to find out who they are. They see themselves reflected back in their activities and the attitudes of those with whom they come in contact. Their circle may be small, but it is important. They will believe the influential people in their lives; if parents tell a child he is stupid, he will likely believe that. If they tell him he is kind and funny, he will believe that. Children's view of themselves is established in part from what parents tell them. Their identity is their assessment of their abilities and characteristics. They define themselves and develop self-esteem dependent on that definition.[8]

While all children need reassurance that they are loved and wanted, adopted children need a great deal more throughout childhood and adolescence.[9] As parents, we can feel as if we are constantly pouring love into a deep well without any evidence it makes any difference. Separations may be especially difficult. The toddler who cries when parents leave becomes the eight-year-old child who is upset if parents are late picking her up from school, and grows into the teen who doesn't want to leave home or go away for a weekend and who insists on knowing where everyone in the family is at all times. It helps to talk to teens about this behaviour as normal for adopted children and something they need to be aware of. Often parents understand their child's yearning for reassurance without realizing that it is common in adopted children.

Establishing a sense of self may be more difficult for adoptees, but a loving family usually provides the continual reassurance they may need and helps the child come to her teen years with a strong sense of self.

Becoming an individual within a group

It is when they hit the task of identity development in adolescence that adoptees can veer widely from the path of non-adopted teens.[10] All teens need to acknowledge their sense of self while at the same time identifying with their peer groups. They want their clothes to reflect their affiliations and their music and their language to be different from their parents and from other groups of teens. Adoptees can find this process of identification difficult if they don't see themselves reflected in their peer group, perhaps because they are of a different race. They may feel that they don't belong to their peer group because they don't have information about their origins and ancestors and so don't feel genuine. It may be difficult, but they need friends in their peer group because, at some point, they need to identify with a group.

If teens feel secure and supported at home, if they have a strong and reliable sense of self, they can successfully accomplish the task of integrating firmly in society. They need to be sure of themselves, sure of the way they interact with others in order to belong to society without losing their individual identity and without denying their family. When they can't do this, they may remain at this stage, seeking identity, continually trying to resolve this over and over for many years.

Their next task, which occurs in the late teens or early adulthood, is to retain their strong individual sense of self while sharing intimacy with another, both in friendship and romantic relationships. We all know someone who is stuck at this stage. They either withdraw when a relationship starts to get intimate, betray it, or sabotage it. Or they may be needy and demanding beyond what a partner or friend can tolerate and so subvert the relationship.

If our children do not resolve these challenges to their identity in a timely manner, they may have difficulty well into adulthood and may react to their fears and anxieties in ways that don't promote a full and rich life. It doesn't mean that they can never successfully resolve these identity tasks—they may do so much later—but they will lead a happier and more productive life if they can deal with these challenges at the appropriate time. Parents can help if we are aware of what the teens are facing and make opportunities for counselling or consulting with mentors when the adoptees need them.

When our friends with biological children send their children off to college, they feel as if their child-rearing days are behind them. We adoptive parents know that we must be on high alert and continue to parent until the identity and intimacy development is completed—and that might be years yet.

Separating from Family

One of the tasks for teens in their search for a secure identity is to remain firmly connected to their families while moving into the broader world of society. The separation occurs in a patchy way that can frustrate parents who see a loving child one day and one that pushes them away the next. Parents can feel unsure of the relationship and bewildered by it. It helps to realize that teens are trying to find their place in society.

Many niches of society are accepting of adopted children. If the child is the same race, the fact that he or she is adopted is not obvious and prejudice is not likely. Extended families often have adopted children in their near relations, and today more families have opened up to accept stepchildren as families blend. Complicated family constellations occur and are fairly common. Families adapt and create the relationships that seem to work for them, and extended families and most people in our modern society understand that this occurs.

Usually, in transracial families, the family members can be so accustomed to the difference in appearance they don't even see it. The Caucasian sister of a Native teenager told me about the racial differences between her and her brother: "It never occurred to me until one day I was introducing my brother to someone, and I suddenly thought that they might think it odd that we had different-coloured skin. Until that time, I'd never thought about it. He was just that colour. Like I had blue eyes and he had brown. I was eighteen, and, hey, I'm pretty smart, but it was only then that I noticed we were different."[11]

Recognition of such differences can and does occur much earlier. Some children are made aware of the difference early, and prejudice may be more easily handled if the child and his siblings know it may happen and are prepared for it. Colour-blindness may not serve the adoptee or the family well.

Need for Adoptive Mother

In spite of the theories of Freud and many other psychiatrists and psychologists, adopted children need to stay close to their adopted mothers. In the past it was commonly believed that boys work through their Oedipal complexes in order to become men. This means that they must repudiate their mother and take their place with other men. The societal pressure on boys in the teen years to distance themselves from their mothers in order to become masculine can create a huge conflict for an adopted boy.[12] If he successfully distances himself from his adoptive mother, he has experienced two fundamental losses—his birth mother and his adopted mother. North Americans in particular seem to emphasize rejection of the mother as a necessary component of manhood. Some psychiatrists say that this process is an innate psychic one that occurs without any social demands. Since many other cultures do not share this process, it is more likely to be socially constructed than a universal process that arises from an intrinsic male need to be autonomous.[13] The very difficulty of the process, the tremendous psychic pain that this effort to separate causes, ought to alert us to the fact that such a separation is not good for anyone. It makes the confusion that adopted teen boys often experience much more understandable.[14] Society's approval of a mother staying close to her son would allow her to love him without feeling she is emasculating him.

Girls are not required to reject their mothers in the same way as boys in our society. In fact, they are expected to love and care for their mothers their whole lives. In the twenty-first century, the notion of masculine and feminine is much broader than in Freud's time. Today, we see "masculine" moving along a continuum that doesn't demand boys fit into rigid limits.

Need for Adoptive Father

I was impressed with the depth of teens' need for their fathers when I researched my first book on teen suicide. I interviewed thirty teens and found that twenty-seven of them had poor relationships with their fathers. They wanted a good relationship, but they didn't have it. It seemed that just as they entered their teen years and needed their fathers, they were abandoned by them.

For some decades, psychologists have emphasized the mother's role in the child's life, but fathers are now being studied more. Two-career families demand more child care from fathers, and peer pressure to spend time with their children also positively influences them. This will, no doubt, result in emotionally healthier children as researchers find that fathers contribute greatly to a child's emotional stability. According to some studies,[15] adoptive fathers are emotionally closer to their children than non-adoptive fathers—an assertion that needs more study to try to determine what aspect of fathering adoptive fathers emphasize. Some aspects of fathering seem to be of particular importance for adoptees. Mothers and others influence children as well, but this section of the book is all about Dad.

Reliability

A child who may have abandonment issues needs to know that you will show up when you say you will—as tardiness causes him or her anxiety—and that you will fulfil your promises. Anything less than reliability can create insecurity and chronic anxiety in the child.

Affection

Dads model affection between partners. Dads who obviously love their partners create a feeling of security in the family. With that affection comes a willingness to work out problems. When dads show both boys and girls how to resolve conflicts in a calm and appropriate way, they are showing, through all the drama of family life, how to accept love and affection from others. They also show the child by a reasonable and supportive approach that violence and abuse are not an option.

To model social behaviour

Fathers introduce their children to the social world outside the family and show them how to act with adults, how to make introductions and respond to them, how to make appropriate conversation, how to stay calm in emotionally charged situations, and how to deal with racial prejudice and still maintain self-respect. In previous generations, fathers were considered to be doing their duty if they provided financially for their children and left much of the social education of their children to the mothers. However, even in those days, fathers, by example, showed children how to act. Today, fathers are more conscious of their need to be involved emotionally and socially in the lives of their children and act as guides to the world outside the home.[16]

Discipline

Fathers in many cultures are the disciplinarians. This can mean that they are the arbitrator of behaviour, but in many modern homes mothers and fathers share this duty. Discipline is not punishment. Fathers need to develop ways to insist on family values without threats or abuse. A father must work at first controlling his own emotions before dealing with his children. Reacting in anger with a loud voice or active hands will not change a child's behaviour. Such fathers are, after all, only showing that the biggest person gets to hit. We need and expect fathers to be loving, not violent.

Security

Fathers who have cared for their child for years create an expectation that Dad will always be there, that he will look after and protect them. Such fathers not only protect their children from poverty by providing what the child needs to survive and prosper, but insist on fair opportunities for their child. They hold the back of the bike on that first foray without training wheels, attend myriad soccer games, and show up at the principal's office when their amazing child does something stupid. Most fathers do not need instructions on how to protect and provide. It is a cultural norm. Fathers expect to do this and usually take pride in it.

Adopted children need this security. With a sense of family security, children can grow and develop. With a father who has an affectionate and loving relationship with his partner, who is reliable, who introduces them to the outside world and offers security, children have a role model that will be their template for healthy living.

Diversity and LGBTQ Parents

LGBTQ parents, single parents, grandparents, and parents of differing races are now encouraged and accepted in North American society. Broader acceptance of diversity among adoptive parents has developed so that many who could not adopt in the past can now do so. While not all social agencies accept diversity, the trend is growing.

There is increasing acceptance of LGBTQ adoptive parents, although there are barriers in some jurisdictions. Research shows that children placed in gay and lesbian families are as well-adjusted and happy as those placed in heterosexual homes.[17] It's possible the media encourages understanding and acceptance of LGBTQ families. A recent television show of the "house hunters" variety featured a gay couple looking for the perfect house to buy so they could adopt a child and start a family. It normalized their need so that viewers, especially those without LGBTQ friends or family members in this community, could appreciate it. Viewers may be influenced by observing, even on TV, the goals and aspirations that are common to all parents. The acceptance of LGBTQ adoptive parents by agencies means that more children will find homes. From a purely practical point of view, adoption agencies need to encourage LGBTQ parents to adopt.

Gay fathers

There is a growing group of LBGTQ adoptive parents who are working out their roles with their adopted children. Same-sex couples seem to have well-adjusted adopted children.[18] In a British study, gay fathers were rated psychologically healthier than heterosexual parents and showed less evidence of stress[19] This report incited wild speculations in my mind: Did gay couples talk more about their feelings and so were able to de-stress? Were they more insightful because they had had to face social oppression? The study didn't say. Another study of adoptive parents' stress and their children's adjustment produced the interesting results that gay parents showed greater warmth and responsiveness to their children, interacted more, and were less aggressive with their children than heterosexual parents.[20] The children of gay parents were less hyperactive but showed no difference in sex-type behaviour. Boys and girls of gay parents acted much the same as boys and girls of heterosexual parents.

Since gay parents tend to receive children from more difficult backgrounds and with challenging behaviours,[21] [22] and since they appear to have better-than-average results in raising children, we may need to study the qualities that achieve those results. We may learn much about parenthood from them.

Lesbian mothers

Adoptees can be placed in two-mother homes. Some lesbian parents include the biological parent with her partner as the adopting parent. In some families, both parents are adoptive parents. This is legal in Canada now and in some states in the US.[23] Myths and fears around the placement of children with lesbian couples have been addressed by studies that show adopted children of these parents to be no more likely to be gay or lesbian than children of heterosexual couples and are essentially no different in development or accomplishment than children of heterosexual parents.[24]

Adoptive lesbian parents usually have taken agency-sponsored classes about adoption, possibly LGBTQ-specific classes, have examined their own feelings, made a family plan, and prepared themselves as much as possible. Lesbian parents will likely have considered their own capabilities as parents, the support (or lack of it) from extended families, and the social stigma their children may face. These adoptive parents may have been prepared for many events, but they still meet the unexpected. In 2015, for example, a family with two mothers and a son was not considered "family" by a US Border guard.[25] There are still areas of both Canada and the US where prejudice against same-sex couples is prevalent. Some states, such as Mississippi and Utah, ban adoption by same-sex parents.[26]

We can hope intrepid lesbian parents continue to find children who need homes and continue to provide support, love, opportunities, and family to children who need them. There are many online resources for same-sex couples and forums that offer support and advice. While every couple's experience is different—some receive their child in a straightforward, albeit nerve-wracking, emotional process, and others have disappointments and struggles in their journey to be parents—it is a journey that results in a family. And that's what all adoptive parents want.

Racial Identity

Adoptees also have to negotiate relationships with extended family members and the greater society to establish their identity. Racial affiliation is part of the identity package.

Transracial adoption gained acceptance after the civil rights movement. But it isn't enough that parents are delighted with their children. The obvious differences of race in a family still require a high level of awareness and specific coping skills. Adoptive parents have reasonable motives for adopting internationally: children may be difficult to find locally; more infants are available internationally; and parents may want a closed adoption. It surprised me that so many of those adopting internationally preferred a closed adoption (fifty-one percent). The adoptee's inability to find information easily about birth parents in a closed adoption may cause difficulties as he or she grows; it is hard for a child to deal with that lack of knowledge. Parents must plan for this.

Many who could not adopt in the past can do so now as broader acceptance of diversity in families developed. However, particularly in the US, not all states and agencies have policies that encourage diversity, and agencies can find it difficult to place some children, particularly black children. The entrenched racism in some parts of American society contributes to the placement of black children out of the country. Adoptive parents in countries more tolerant of racial diversity than the US can apply to adopt a US-born child, and a stream of American children is now exported. Most go to Canada and to European countries such as the Netherlands and the United Kingdom where racial prejudice is arguably less strong.[27] This seems ironic. On the one hand, US adoptive parents go abroad to find adoptable children while, at the same time, social agencies export adoptable children. We can turn this around with a change in policies, making racial matching a low priority in placement. This would make it possible for more domestic adoptions.

With a change in policies, and by encouraging diverse communities such as the LGBTQ community, single men and women, and older parents to adopt, more domestic adoptions can be made possible. Of course, acceptance of all races as equal is still the ideal.

Race and culture

P.W. Jackson, a noted psychologist, talks about culture as something that is "established by shared knowledge of a set of well-known stories. Lacking that knowledge, a person is unable to participate fully in the social community to which he or she belongs."[29] Cultural differences can exist among members of the same race. In British Columbia, where I live, there are at least thirty-four different Native languages,[30] so one assumes at least thirty-four different cultures, as language holds the culture. While we may be eager and willing to adopt the culture of our child's heritage and find ways for her to understand and be part of it, we first have to learn which culture in her race is most appropriate for her. Participating fully in the social community is key, but it is often very hard for adopted children to do. Adoptees may lack the shared stories of the culture, but they can attain some comfort with their own race.

Affirming racial identity

Pressures to fit in and to find a group where they feel accepted become important in the teen or young adult's life; belonging to one's family is no longer enough. For transracial adoptees, that can mean belonging to a racially similar group. If parents have established connections with same-race groups and individuals, the teen's transition to a same-race group can be fairly straightforward.

It is an instructive experience to participate with your child in their racial group. I was once a guest at a wedding where there were 500 Native people and one non-Native white—me. I was very conscious of my skin. Everyone was polite and welcoming. But I felt strange. I knew most people were aware of my relationship with my son. His birth mother was at the wedding and we were on friendly terms, but I was a guest and an outsider, an *amsiiwa*, in their language. I began to understand how my son felt in white society.

I couldn't, however, know exactly how he felt. I rarely read instant rejection in the body language of people I meet, experienced lowered expectations or unfair persecution—experiences that are common for many non-white people in North American society. I don't have to decide every day which overt prejudicial act I will respond to, which I will ignore, and which I will simply suffer because it is too dangerous to respond. This negotiation of prejudice is a dance with society that our different-race children must learn. We can help by introducing them to a mentor, an admired older person of their own race who has successfully dealt with society, and by joining groups where their race is either the majority or, at least, has a strong minority status. Internet forums can be useful, but as a source of embittered railing against unfairness, although justified, they can be hard on your child. Such forums do show that others feel the injustice of prejudice, and fate hasn't picked your child out to be a martyr. It can be comforting. Hearing others complain about prejudice can normalize your child's reaction, help him or her to see that others have these feelings, and make dealing with them easier. It can also make their situation look hopeless. Internet forums need to be chosen carefully for an elementary-school child and discussed in depth with a teen.

I grew up where I never saw racial prejudice. I lived in an

almost completely white neighbourhood, and my parents appeared respectful of people of different races when we met them in the city. I was unprepared for racism. I began to see it when I moved north into a rural area and worked as a public health nurse. There was one system of health care for white people and another for Native people. There was a Catholic church for whites and another for Natives. I found it amazing and appalling. I subverted the health care system when I could. For instance, I refused to give different vaccines based on race, worked with the chief of a local reserve to get getter health care, and began to see, in this rural community, how entrenched racism was. I met Native friends for coffee and great conversations, but I was not invited to their homes and they rarely came to mine. We negotiated our friendships carefully—and such friendships were rare in this town. I had one Native friend who was integrated into white society, but I am sure that most people did not realize she was Native. She never mentioned it. That should have prepared me for prejudice when I adopted my son, but somehow I was naïve about it. It took years of paying attention, looking over his shoulder, and noticing reactions before I realized prejudice was alive and offensive. I was surprised that teachers, professionals that they are, would be prejudiced, but we met them. Luckily, my son knew he was intelligent and accomplished and regarded those teachers as idiots. It isn't easy to keep that attitude in the larger context of white society.

It is important to fully realize that your child is a different race. I know that sounds obvious, but I clearly remember wondering if my neighbour's baby was sick because she was so pale and then realizing I thought my own brown boy was the norm. You get used to seeing your child, and you don't necessarily see his race first—in fact, you rarely see his race first.

As children grow, the concept of race becomes more important.

We need to help them find a racial identity, but first they need a strong family identity. It must be clear to them that they do not need to give up one identity to attain the other. They can be both members of a family, secure in their position, as well as members of a racial group. It is important for adoptive parents to help their children deal with their racial identity because their concern about it doesn't go away as they age. Effects of adoption and specifically transracial adoption can, and often do, persist into adulthood. There must be a resolution or an accommodation of the feelings around adoption and racial identity for your child to find peace.

Pre-adoption classes for transracial families explore the ways in which parents can help their child increase a sense of belonging in their racial group. They offer advice on how to make connections to birth families, group affiliations, and other transracial adoptive families and set up ways to facilitate this. Grab those connections.

I wish a book such as Beth Hall and Gail Steinberg's *Inside Transracial Adoption*[30] had been published years ago. Rather than gain knowledge through painful observations and experiences, I could have learned much by reading their advice.

Being the parent of a different-race child

People do ask the most ignorant and ridiculous questions. My favourite was, "Can he speak Indian?" I was asked this when my son was about four years old. I was flummoxed. Who asks that kind of question? Because our children are obviously different, people can be curious, critical, prejudiced, or nosy, and they don't mind sharing their ignorance. They do make us pay attention to how we see ourselves as parents. We need to develop our own identities as parents of a transracial family.

One of the ways we do that is to normalize the experience.

We can seek out other parents of transracial families and talk. We can put ourselves in the position of being the minority in our children's racial groups. We can find a mentor who knows how to recognize and deal with prejudice. There is a trick in knowing when to challenge racism and when to slide away from it. We can listen to our child tell us how she copes with it and what it means to her. We can try some of her strategies and talk about whether they were useful. We can be easy with our position and with our child's position in the world and surround ourselves with others who are relaxed with our family. What we cannot do is pretend we are all one race. It's a fine line between denying our family looks any different from most families and displaying ourselves as the model of diversity. We need to reach a comfortable social position. My own view is that our family is both richer for its composition and normal for us. It is neither better nor worse for its diversity; it just is.

EXAMINING OUR OWN VIEW OF RACE

As we accept our child's race as part of our family structure, we need to become more knowledgeable about it. Not everyone does what I did and takes a PhD that involves field work in their son's community. And I wouldn't say that was the best way to understand it. A PhD thesis is, by its nature, a narrow look at a subject and lacks emotional input. I was lucky in that my previous work on suicide prevention and public health experience was valued by my son's community, and so they talked to me. That didn't make me a member of that community; it just gave me a chance to learn about it.

You may seek birth relatives or even a community group that is organized around your child's ethnic and racial heritage. Interaction with people of his race forces you to examine your own attitudes. No one is without prejudice of some kind. We use stereotypes to organize thought, after all; it's a normal cognitive skill. What we aren't always aware of is how stereotypical thinking keeps us from understanding individuals. Interaction with individuals of another race can shove those stereotypes into our conscious thought. We need those interactions to deepen our understanding of our child's heritage and our attitude toward it—and it is necessary to examine our attitude. Our view of their race will come out in our speech and body language. Children are astute at reading our bodies. They will know what we think and feel.

Can We Provide the Love Our Children Need?

We can try. When we understand our children's needs, the task of providing for them can seem monumental. We know good parents who have problem children. The choices kids face today may confuse us and the "right" way may seem a somewhat slippery concept. How do we enjoy our children while guiding them to a happy life?

Luckily, we aren't expected to do everything at once. We accomplish the day-by-day tasks and come up with spur-of-the-moment responses as our children require them. It helps if we have absorbed all that information the adoption agency supplied, the reading we have done, and the advice we received from others so that our responses satisfy the needs of our children.

We do depend on love for our children to help smooth the way. Love is a power in our families. In quantum physics, "entanglement" is a foundational concept. A family constellation is certainly a form of "entanglement." According to Ronald Hamm, holistic veterinarian and author, "Loving, giving, and the altruistic intent to heal another are all products of mindful process, and their physical manifestations are fundamentally indistinguishable [from the mental intention]."[32]

According to quantum physics, subatomic particles only materialize upon observation. I translate that to mean you can manifest what you concentrate on. If we concentrate on love, then we can create love. I realize that I have an imperfect understanding of quantum physics and this is an oversimplification, but it does seem that those who visualize an outcome are more likely to achieve it.

Adoptive parents aren't perfect parents. We make many of the same mistakes all parents make. We have the same moral dilemmas of discipline and leniency and the conundrum of how much control to exert over our children's lives, but we are much better prepared now than in the past to cope with the adoption-induced problems of abandonment and alienation. And, like most parents, we are hopeful that we can find the courage, skills, and understanding we need to provide a nurturing, loving home for our kids. We're resilient; we're optimists.

1   Andrea Chatwin, "Attachment and Adoption Webinar." Adoptive Families Association of BC. (Vancouver, May 5, 2015.)

2   Marion Crook, *The Face in the Mirror: Teens and Adoption* (Vancouver: Arsenal Pulp Press, 2000), 56.

3   Ibid., 57.

4   Malcolm Hill, Anne Stafford, Peter Seaman, Nicola Ross, and Brigid Daniel, *Parenting and Resilience*. (New York: Joseph Roundtree Foundation, 2007.)

5   Femmie Juffer and Marinus H. van Ijzendoorn, "Adoptees Do Not Lack Self-Esteem: A Meta-Analysis of Studies on Self-Esteem of Transracial, International, and Domestic Adoptees," *APA PsychNet: American Psychological Association Psychological Bulletin* 133 (6) 2007: 1067-1083. http://dx.doi.org/10.1037/0033-2909.133.6.1067

6   "The Road to Resilience," American Psychological Association. APA Help Center [No date]. http://www.jrf.org.uk/sites/files/jrf/parenting-resilience-children.pdf or http://www.apa.org/helpcenter/road-resilience.aspx

7   Crook, *The Face in the Mirror*, 101.

8   Angela Oswalt and C.E. Zupanick, eds., "The Development of Self-Identity." Seven Counties Service. Louisville, KY. [No date.] http://www.amhc.org/1310-child-development-theory-adolescence-12-24/article/41162-the-development-of-self-identity

9   Crook, *The Face in the Mirror*, 100.

10   S.A. McLeod, "Erik Erikson," *Simply Psychology* 2008, updated 2013. http://simplypsychology.org/Erik-Erikson.html

11   Crook, *The Face in the Mirror*, 92.

12   Ibid., 98.

13   William Pinar, personal communication cited in Marion Crook, *The Face in the Mirror*, 98.

14   Ibid.

15   Rosa Rosnati and Daniela Barni, "Being a Father: A Comparison Between Adoptive and Non-Adoptive Families with School-Aged Children," *Children* 93, no. 144: 2006. http://citeseerx.ist.psu.edu/viewdoc/download?doi=10.1.1.557.8250&rep=rep1&type=pdf

16   Jeffrey Rosenberg and W. Bradford Wilcox, *The Importance of Fathers in the Health Development of Children*. (Abuse and Neglect User Manual Series.) (Washington, DC: US Department of Health and Human Services, Administration for Children and Families, Children's Bureau. 2006.) http://childwelfare.gov/pubPDFs/fatherhood.pdf

17   David M. Brodzinsky, "Expanding Resources for Children III. Research-based Best Practices in Adoption by Gays and Lesbians." The Evan B. Donaldson Adoption Institute, October, 2011. http://adoptioninstitute.org/old/publications/2011_10_Expanding_Resources_BestPractices_ExecSumm.pdf

18   Charlotte J Patterson, *Lesbian and Gay Adoption: Looking Ahead* (Charlottesville, VA: Hunter College Center for LGBT Social Science & Public Policy, University of Virginia, 2010.) http://.hunter.cuny.edu/socwork/nrcfcpp/info_services/download/Patterson.HunterCollege.October2010.pdf

19   Susan Golombok, Laura Mellish, Sarah Jennings, Polly Casey, Fiona Tasker, and Michael E. Lamb, "Adoptive Gay Father Families: Parent-Child Relationships and Children's Psychological Adjustment." *Child Development* 85 (2) (2014), 456-468. http://onlinelibrary.wiley.com/doi/10.1111/cdev.12155/epdf

20   Ibid.

21   David M. Brodzinsky cited in Golombok, et al, "Adoptive Gay Father Families," 457.

22   Rosnati and Barni, "Being a Father." http://citeseerx.ist.psu.edu/viewdoc/download?doi=10.1.1.557.8250&rep=rep1&type=pdf

23   Lina Guillen, "Gay and Lesbian Adoption and Parenting: The Legal Rights Of Same-Sex Parents, from Adoption to Coparenting to Second Parent Rights." *NOLO Law for All.* [no date] http://nolo.com/legal-encyclopedia/gay-lesbian-adoption-parenting-29790.html

24   "Gay and Lesbian Adoptive Parents: Resources for Professionals and Parents." (Washington, DC: NAIC National Adoption Information Clearinghouse, April 2000.) http://childwelfare.gov/pubPDFs/f_gay.pdf

25   Siobhan Rowe, "Academy of Pediatrics Supports Adoption by Same Sex Parents," *Focus on Adoption Magazine.* Adoptive Families Association of BC, August 5, 2013. http://bcadoption.com/print/190

26   Rhonda Payne, "Unexpected Challenges," *Focus on Adoption Magazine.* Adoptive Families Association of BC, January 5, 2015. http://bcadoption.com/resources/articles/unexpected-challenges

27   Guillen, "Gay and Lesbian Adoption and Parenting."

28   Rebecca Buckwalter-Poza, "America's Unseen Export: Children, Most of Them Black," *Pacific Standard,* June 24, 2014. http://psmag.com/politics-and-law/outgoing-adoption-americas-unseen-export-children-black-84084

29   Phillip W. Jackson in Hunter McEwan and Kieran Egan, *Narrative in Teaching, Learning and Research* (New York, London: Teachers College Press, 1995), 5.

30   "Culture and Language." Province of British Columbia. [No date] http://www2.gov.bc.ca/gov/content/governments/aboriginal-people/supporting-communities/culture-language

31   Beth Hall and Gail Steinberg, *Inside Transracial Adoption: Strength-Based, Culture-Sensitizing, Parenting Strategies for Inter-Country or Domestic Adoptive Families That Don't "Match"* (London and Philadelphia: Jessica Kingsley Publishers, 2013).

32   Ronald Hamm, *The Philosophic Foundation of Holistic Medicine: The Deductions* ([n.l.]: Ronald Hamm, 2010), 318.

6 Helping Adoptees through Ages and Stages

Adoptive parents could benefit from a degree in child development and a thorough understanding of psychology. We have this notion that if we only go to another class, read another book, or talk to another wise person, we could understand what we need to know. It all helps, but there is no such thing as perfection in parenthood. Everyone has their own parenting style. I intellectualized every problem and ignored feelings. I finally learned to research a problem, ask advice, and *then* go with my instincts. The results were much better than striving to understand every nuance of my child's behaviour. I still research and talk to advisors, but I also pay attention and try to respond emotionally. Some adoptive parents figure out their parenting style before the child is in the house, but most of us learn as we go.

When we don't know what to expect as our children grow, we may be afraid of what's coming. It helps to have some idea of how being adopted affects our children as they mature.

Newborns and Infants

I graduated from university in nursing at a time when medical personnel and parents knew babies needed to be held, comforted, and fed when they wanted to be—not necessarily on Mom's schedule—and their cries were their way of communicating. Parents were there to satisfy the baby's needs. Parents, for the most part, were committed to hauling babies around, keeping them close, feeding them, getting up with them at night, and generally giving them care and attention.

When my children were small, there were—and I believe, still are—very few general practitioners or public health nurses who understood the particular needs of adopted babies. We got advice about babies, but not advice about *adopted* babies. Today, the best source of information about our children is likely our local adoptive parents' organization. The medical world is a good place for information about normal physical and intellectual growth and development, but other adoptive parents might be a better source of information about the particular behaviour, sleep, feeding, and cuddling patterns that often accompany adopted children. When adopted babies are working out their separation trauma, they can refuse to cuddle, react hysterically when separated from adopted parents, refuse to eat if fed by anyone but the adopted mother, wail at night if placed in a room away from adopted parents, and exhibit other signs of separation trauma. It helps to understand that this is the way your newborn is trying to adjust.

Parents of newborns are immersed in the minutiae of bottles, spilled formula, burps, smiles, cuddles, bags of diapers, broken sleep, and snatched meals. Underlying this constant activity is our responsibility to give this child the best chance we can for his or her happiness.

Emotional nurturing

At this age, the baby's physical needs must be met. As well, the child's emotional needs must be satisfied in order to build a sense of trust.

We know about the separation of the child from the birth mother and the consequent trauma of that separation.[1] The transition to the new home of the adoptive parents may be at the moment of birth, when the adoptive parents are there to catch the baby, or a few days, weeks, or years later, when the child comes to the new home. In all cases, we expect the child will suffer some kind of disruption and will need to be encouraged to bond strongly with the adoptive parents.

If we had the experience of loving, affectionate parents in a family in which babies were carried constantly, we may find providing nurturing to our new child is quite easy. But many didn't come from homes where there were hordes of children, and this baby may be our first experiment with mothering or fathering. We can be highly anxious and insecure. It's hard to provide security and a calm atmosphere when we haven't experienced it ourselves. We aren't really sure what normal parenting is. A mentor is helpful here—a neighbour, a friend, or a relative whose parenting style we admire and whose kids seemed to turn out just fine. Adoptive parenting groups can be a reliable resource, especially if the parents in the group have several children and aren't stumbling around the way we are.

Many adopted infants require post-traumatic care. They have differing reactions to separation from their birth mothers, some more severe than others, but we can assume all will have some kind of response. The children must have a reliable closeness to their adoptive parents. This could include the skin-to-skin "kangaroo care" that promotes emotional attachment. This kind of contact was first found to benefit premature infants.[2] Mothers are so attuned to their infants when they hold them close like this; they even adjust their body temperature in response to their child's. This is not a style of infant care most of us experienced ourselves or even observed. It has been recommended for years for parents of pre-term infants, for infants who have experienced trauma, and now for multiple-birth infants.[3] It seems a good idea for adopted infants as well. Apparently, those marvellous babies will also sync their heart rate to their adopted mother's, so biologically, the new mother and baby are connected.[4]

The summer before my youngest son was born, the family—my husband and two children aged six and five, and me—loaded into our camper and headed for a six-week trip to the Yukon. We picked up a small kitten from a neighbour as we were leaving and brought her with us. Because she was a little young to leave her mother, we kept her warm by tucking her down into one or another of our shirts. We took turns, and someone always had "Missy" snuggled on their chest. Once, when we all got out of the truck at a café stop, one of the kids noticed kitten legs hanging out the bottom of my husband's shirt. He was so accustomed to having her close, he had forgotten her. We caught her before she fell. She spent six weeks cuddled up that way. We returned home from our trip in time for the birth of our youngest son. Even after our experience with Missy, it never occurred to any of us to tuck a nine-pound, seven-and-a-half-ounce baby into our shirts. We should have.

The reassurance we can give our infants—whether through skin-to-skin contact, immediate response to their distress cries, or by constantly holding and cuddling them and communicating through coos and goos and other gentle vocalizations—results in greater attachment, which, in turn, results in the child's greater ability to trust others. The sense of trust is a necessary development in the healthy emotional life of our children.

Infants seem to convey their wants directly. They usually cry; we respond. They need to cuddle; so do we. It's a simple communication system. It gets more complex as the child ages.

Talking about adoption

Some authors, such as Beth Hall and Gail Steinberg,[5] advocate talking to your baby, even a tiny baby, about adoption and, if trans-racial, about race. Their reasoning is: you will get used to talking about it, and the words will come more naturally and more easily when the child is older. I didn't know this when my son was young.

When my youngest was five, he attended kindergarten for only half a day. The other half-day, he and I went adventuring. One day, we drove to the local Native reserve to arrange with Mrs. B., who was a member of that nation, to transport her boar to our sow on the ranch. We wanted piglets, and she had the boar. The price was probably a couple of the resulting piglets.

She looked at my son and said, "Is he one of the Gilberts?"—a local Native family. I was quite indignant. "No, he's mine," I said. She apologized and I suddenly realized she had a legitimate point. I was the one who wasn't paying attention here. I explained his band affiliation and his nation. She nodded. Obviously, I should have practiced my response beforehand. Talking to my son when he was an infant might have made it easier to deal with questions.

It may not be as valuable to the children to hear their adoption story and stories of their race before they can understand them, but it may make adoptive parents better at talking about it. This is the time in their lives where we, their parents, must become easy with our adoptive status and, if applicable, our different race. Practice can contribute to ease, so we need to create opportunities to talk with our children—not constantly, but enough so it is a relaxed conversation.

Toddlers

Is our three-year-old throwing her toys at the wall because she is a normal three-year-old and doesn't do impulse-control very well? Or is she suffering from lack of trust, post-traumatic stress, primal wound effects, or fear of attachment? Is this normal assertiveness, parental ineptitude, or a symptom of deep stress? If this is our first child, it can be hard to know. If it's our third child, it might be easier, but there are no guarantees here. Sometimes the third baffles us.

Some of the advice professionals give us is easy to follow: "Keep them close." That's not hard. Even when both parents work outside the home, we are usually aware our children need us physically present as much as possible, and we want that. In fact, we have the roaming parental eye most of the time, constantly checking our child's whereabouts. Keeping them close seems normal. What is more difficult is mastering the complex skills necessary to raise a thoughtful, considerate child instead of a self-indulgent monster. Which boundaries do we insist on, which do we let slide? If we have consistent rules, children find it easier to obey than if the rules change day to day. If they know what is expected, they are more likely to cooperate. Still, they will test us.

Discipline

Adopted parents must consider what kind of discipline they are going to use in order to teach their child how to live in a family and in the world. If our child has come from an abusive situation, we will probably avoid any discipline that involves touch, even pulling them or putting a hand on them to guide them. Children who have been left alone for hours in a former situation will panic if we use a "time-out in your bedroom" disciplinary tactic. The old method of sitting on a low chair or a step on inside stairs might work for children who fear abandonment, and that, we can assume, is most adopted children. A minute of sitting for each year—three minutes for a three-year-old, four minutes for a four-year-old—might be effective. We can work out before the infraction occurs how to discipline and teach our child without traumatizing him or her.

Every confrontation seems a moral dilemma. Parenting is not for moral cowards. Parenting classes and adoptive parenting associations may offer post-adoption support groups that can be very helpful. We have the usual problems of all parents about how to teach without imposing the discipline of an army camp as well as how adjust to the sensitivities of adopted children who fear abandonment.

Talking about adoption

Most of us tell our children they are adopted. We have some simple story when they are toddlers that becomes more detailed as they grow.[6] It isn't necessary to include all the details until the child is old enough to deal with them, as some events in their past may be hard for them to accept. Transracial children need to be aware they are different from their parents before they are questioned about it on the playground. It is important to normalize their appearance, in the same way we would normalize different-coloured eyes: "We just come that way." Like the adoption story, this discussion of race becomes more detailed as they age.

At the same time as our transracial child sees differences, he should see people of his same race in his social sphere so he doesn't think he is the only one in the world who has dark skin or light skin. We can provide books and toys that show characters with varied shades of skin colour. It is easier now than it was in the past to find action figures or dolls that are of the same race as our child. I remember standing in front of a floor-to-ceiling wall of dolls and shaking my head in frustration. "Not one brown doll!" I complained. A woman beside me said, "I can't find what I want either." I turned and discovered she was of Asian descent. We were looking at a wall of blonde, blue-eyed white dolls. It was one of those times I was ashamed to have been so oblivious to white bias.

It takes effort at times to create a world in which our child's adoption story is comfortable for them, and at the same time truthful and supportive. And it takes effort to make a transracial child's story fit into the wider story of our society. If a child has been severely traumatized before adoption, then professional help at the toddler stage is necessary. A toddler is normally reactive, assertive, and contrary. That child who throws herself on the floor of the grocery store and screams for ice cream may be yours. Children do that on occasion. Adopted children have additional stresses, and their behaviour and severe reactions can sometimes seem inexplicable to us. Children who suffered trauma may react to certain stimuli in a way parents don't understand. When we don't understand, we can look for support and advice.

Elementary School Age

Whether you have had six weeks or six years with your child, school-aged children can give you new and sometimes nerve-wracking experiences. They will climb on roofs, explore old cellars, blurt out family secrets, and fight with siblings. They will also look at the world with wonder and curiosity, ask more questions than you can answer, pout, scream hostilities, be kind to animals, start playground fights, and try out more diverse behaviours than you knew existed. When I had three children in elementary school, I sometimes felt like the goalie at a hockey practice where the whole team was shooting pucks at me and I had to catch every one.

Will adoption affect our child's development through the elementary school-aged years? Well, yes. Somewhat. There are some common tasks children must accomplish in order to be at peace with their adoption during this time. They must understand their adoptive status and have some idea of racial status. How capable are we as parents at meeting our child's needs? Most parents are capable in some areas and not in others. If there are two parents, the chances of covering all the bases are better. If there is just one parent or both parents have deficiencies in the same area, then outside professionals can help.

Feeling loved and appreciated

As adoptive parents we are good at letting our children know they are loved. If we have had our children in our family for many years, we've developed ways to let them know we love them. If they just arrived, we work at developing that love and letting them feel it. Whatever their past, most children have the ability to form a strong attachment.[7] Persevere and it will happen. Affection is easy for some parents to give, and harder for others. If our own background did not include affectionate words or actions, then we must make a conscious effort to develop a style of showing affection. It's rewarding, as children respond to it, but it may take effort at first. If they are severely affected by past trauma, even newborn separation from the birth mother, they may continually thrust our love away because they don't want to risk being abandoned again. We may require help with this. Most children aren't that severely affected and respond to consistent and predictable love and affection.

Elementary school is the age of soccer games, skating, Brownies and Scouts, music lessons, and ethnic dance. As well, there is math homework, piano practice, and sleepovers. Into that busy schedule we also must take time to make eye contact with our child, truly listen to her, and connect emotionally. This requires at least half an hour, one-on-one, with our child every day. If we have three children, where are we going to find an hour and a half to simply listen? It is important.

I once spent a week with an Inuit family on Baffin Island, Nunavut, Canada, 2,000 miles north of the Arctic Circle. Only the teenaged daughter spoke English; the family spoke Inuktitut. It is a language with many silences. There is great emotional connection in those silences. When people of the community spoke English to me, they used the Inuktitut cadence so there were long silences in the conversation. I have never felt so seen, appreciated, and listened to in my life. It is that emotional acceptance that produces relaxation, a feeling that all will be well. We strive for that attentive emotional connection with our children.

Understanding their own adoption story

We have been telling our child for years a simple adoption story. During the elementary school years, we can add details. Some sources recommend a family story book that includes all the members of the family with their particular backgrounds.[8] Since Mom and Dad have different backgrounds, it seems reasonable that a child might bring his or her own background to the family. We can add pieces to the family account as the child ages; more information enriches it as he or she becomes mature enough to understand. As well, we can add more and more people to the narrative as cousins are born and relatives divorce and remarry. As the story becomes richer, our child can see how they are connected to many people. It is fairly simple to create and update such a book on our computers, but children may prefer to hold a "real" book in their hands. You can print a revised edition every few years.

Adopted children will be aware they have two sets of parents and two families, and they must integrate those families into an acceptable whole. It is important for them to see where they fit into that integration. A book about your child's life can help with this.

Children need to be comfortable talking about their adoption without having a family drama. The comfort level seems to depend on us, the parents. Children have inhibitions about when and where to talk about adoption unless we make it easy for them. If we take a deep breath, sit down and gather our courage before we talk about adoption, rest assured, our child will not bring it up very often. If we respond casually, without going into great detail and take the conversation as far as our child wants to go, he or she will probably bring it up again. Perhaps what we need to do most of all is listen when our children want to talk about adoption.

Children learn to explain their adoption when it is appropriate and refuse to explain when it is not. They learn how to answer kind but nosy questions, rude and nosy questions, prejudice, and over-solicitousness. They learn that from us. When we respond to comments about adoption in front of them, we model social behaviour.

Once I was dealing with quite a stupid prank one of my sons had managed to engineer, and my neighbour sympathized, "Well, it's not your fault; he's adopted."

I snapped, "And all four parents are thoroughly ashamed of him at the moment!" How dare he imply my son's heritage was inferior! Really! No one was hurt in his prank; it wasn't any more stupid than most teen behaviour, and I wasn't having his birth parents blamed for it. It probably wasn't a useful response, but even when I didn't know his birth parents, I defended them as part of the family.

We can talk to our child about how we hope she has inherited a talent for music or dance, if that is in her background. We can make connections to the birth family for our child. The biological father of my eldest son was taking math in university. When my son did well in math, I mentioned that he may have inherited a talent for it, although, always the mom, noted he'd have to work to develop it.

This is the phase when we have meetings with the teacher and school principal (and counsellor and special needs teacher, depending on the problem). We can talk about our child's adoption but only in a way that might contribute to their understanding. As always, we look for a reasonable position between avoiding discussion of adoption and talking about it as if it were the complete descriptor of our child. Not everything can be attributed to adoption. Our daughter may have failed her spelling test because she didn't study, not because she is adopted. We set out our expectations for our child and for the teachers. Goal-setting might be useful here, and a follow-up visit to see if the goals were met.

I was impressed with my youngest son's grade-two teacher who had a chart for each child with individual goals in each subject—particular to the child—along with the date she expected him or her to reach those goals. We didn't talk about my son's adoption because he didn't have any trouble learning and she didn't require any explanations.

On the other hand, sometimes our children have learning problems because they are putting so much energy into trying to adjust emotionally to their adoption they have little energy to learn. Then teachers and parents need to talk about it.

Integrating their appearance into their concept of themselves

Some elementary-school children are colour blind, but most see colour differences the way they see size and eye-colour differences—as normal. Some, however, use racial differences as a vehicle for bullying. School staff are less tolerant of this than they used to be, and teachers are more aware they must integrate examples of different races in their teaching. Positive role models are necessary. Not only do our children need to integrate their appearance into their identity, they need to see their appearance as a positive attribute. This can be hard to do if your child's race is considered inferior in your community. A community where his race is accepted and seen as at least equal will help combat the social stigma that comes his way. This is important in the teen years, but the foundations of the child's personal view of race are set in these early years. It's essential to be aware of their experience around this.

Children notice differences in size and weight, hair colour, and physical abilities such as athleticism during these years and for some years to come. Their self-worth can become merged with some of these attributes, such as thinness, and it can take a great deal of time and support to help your child accept their appearance and talents without believing that they are only worthwhile if they fit some different vision of themselves.

This is a good time to check out your own biases; we all have them. How accepting are you of differences? Racial? Physical? Financial? Do you think the poor lack resources because they don't deserve them? Do you think the uneducated are to be ignored? How do you act around those who trigger your prejudices? Admitting to your child you have prejudices can start an illuminating conversation, and it can be a period of great learning for parents.

Establishing a position in the family

If a child was adopted as a newborn, he or she will grow up accustomed to having a certain position in the family. We can solidify that position with references to it such as my eldest son, my youngest daughter, or my one and only. Grandparents, aunts, and uncles can help by accepting the child's birth order. Position does appear to influence the child's view of the world and, to some extent, predict his or her long-range view of their capabilities.[9,10] Not everyone agrees with this. New studies indicate it is less important than we thought.[11] If your child has come from a family where he was a middle child and is suddenly the eldest or youngest, he will have to adjust his view of himself. This can take a great deal of emotional energy. It is usually outside our experience and we may not know how to deal with it. Like many curve balls that come our way, we can deal with it best by listening to our child and encouraging him.

Developing skills

This is the stage when children have an aggressive curiosity and learn at an amazing rate. We provide lessons so they can develop skills. Mastering skills is a source of self-confidence and contributes to the child's feeling of being part of a group. Self-confidence comes with competence, not from parents telling the child how wonderful she is. It comes from accomplishments she has mastered: her ability to play the fiddle allows her to fit in with her fiddle-playing friends; her prowess as a goalie allows her to fit into her soccer team; his batting skills make him important to his baseball team. Similarly, their accomplishments in school make it clear to them just where they fit into the class. What is important to their future is their belief they can master skills now and continue to do so.

Understanding physical growth

Puberty occurs much younger than it did a generation or two ago. Children are hardly ready for it when it is upon them. We can expect to have the "sex talk" much earlier than we did in the past. With early-onset puberty, our children must understand the social restrictions and boundaries around sexuality early in life. It's a bit much for an eight-year-old to absorb, but simplified rules or behaviour guidelines are imperative.

Some parents think they have to talk to their children about menstruation, wet dreams, and sexual intercourse only once. No. It is possible the first time we discuss this or lecture about it, the child doesn't really hear it. It is, after all, a somewhat bizarre story. Who would believe it? In any case, the child thinks her parents couldn't possibly do that. We must return to the conversation several times, add to the explanation, and listen to their questions. It is often uncomfortable or downright scary for the parents. It is easier to pick up on an event, a television incident, an overheard discussion, and start the conversation from that point than to introduce it cold. It still seems early. Children may not be intellectually or socially mature enough to deal with it when puberty arrives.

If we have contact with the birth mother, we may be able to find out at what age her puberty began and perhaps when her brothers matured, but even if we do, apparently environmental influences today create earlier puberty, so the last generation's timing may not be significant.

Differences are celebrated

This is the age when children will ask questions about adoption—that is, if they have sensed you are open to those questions. They will not ask if they fear you will be hurt or will deny their concerns. It is at this stage in their lives they demand answers from you for many things: "Why isn't the teacher fair?" "Why doesn't Grandma like me?" "Why did my birth mother give me away?" "Why didn't anyone in her family want me?" These are legitimate questions—and so hard to answer. Do I answer this truthfully? Do I give some information, but not all? What is she really asking? We do the best we can and, when in doubt, go for honesty and full disclosure. The opposite is worse.

Get down on her level. It is really hard to talk to someone towering over you. Make eye contact and give as honest an answer as you can. Provide reassurance. Practice ahead of time so you use words such as "made a birth plan" instead of "gave you away." Say, "They couldn't take care of any child at that time," instead of "They couldn't keep you."[12] Our language reflects our vision of our child's past, and that should be as helpful as possible.

During this age, children come to believe they cause things to happen. They are good, and good things happen; they are bad, and bad things happen. Being given up for adoption was a bad thing; therefore, they must have caused it to happen. They must have been bad or so different from their birth family, they were not wanted. This is hard to refute because they were given up. At this age, children are unlikely to understand the pressures on their birth mother. An act was good or bad for them, fair or unfair. While they may not express this notion, they may hold a strong feeling they are in some way inferior. They recognize they are different from non-adopted children, and if they are of another race, that difference is obvious. They, therefore, must be inferior. We may have to work very hard to combat this.

Dealing with core issues

You've done everything you can think of, and your child still shows signs of trauma: hoarding food, delayed developmental stages, lying, and fighting. This is where you can use a team. It might consist of you and your partner, a grandmother, the teacher, the doctor, the adoption specialist, or a group from an adoptive families association. If you put effort into dealing with your child's problems now, you may avoid a lot of heartache in the future, and your child will reach peace much sooner. Instead of dealing with individual symptoms of trauma such as lying and, months later, dealing with fighting in the playground, and then, months later, with hoarding food, try to work at the core problem of abandonment or separation trauma. It may be this is motivating your child and you need to put in effort over a concentrated period of time to resolve these issues. The team may be able to pinpoint a habit of yours such as using a "time-out in your bedroom" as discipline instead of "time-out on the kitchen chair." You can change this habit, and it may reassure your child. Perhaps you are in the habit of standing when talking to your child; squatting down to his level might reassure him you are accessible. It sometimes takes an outsider to notice how our habits affect our children. With the focussed assistance of a team, you may be able to make the changes your child needs.

Take care, though, you don't accept the diagnosis of a team that counters your knowledge of your child. One child-assessment expert told me my ten-year-old son had severe hand-eye coordination problems. I thought about that for a moment.

"He goes hunting with his dad, and he can shoot a duck out of the sky. That's hand-eye coordination."

She stared at me. "It is. Excellent hand-eye coordination."

"Let's not tell him he doesn't have it," I said.

We didn't, and he had few problems.

Classroom and schoolyard issues

Teachers can be of tremendous help. They can also be damaging. All I ask of a teacher in elementary school is that he or she be calm, encouraging, pleasant, and accepting. Brilliant would be nice, but not necessary. What I am on the lookout for is the teacher who is angry, judgemental, sarcastic, or forceful. They exist. Some are more concerned about controlling children than teaching them, and it shows in the way the children respond. I used to breathe a sigh of relief at the end of September when my child still liked school.

Volunteer to help the teacher and, if possible, get some in-class time so you can observe the environment. While I would like to assume all teachers are benevolent and devoted to helping our children, it isn't true. Parents must be vigilant. What we do about a poor teaching environment depends on what is possible in our school district. Home-schooling is only for the brave and those without outside-the-home employment. Changing classes might be an option, changing schools another. Enhancing our child's social group so that even in the classroom he feels part of a group might be another way of beefing up our child's ability to deal with difficult teachers. My youngest son belonged to a group of about fifteen boys (soccer players all) who had a solidarity that made them imperviousness to the teachers who yelled or were sarcastic to them. They apparently just stared at the teacher when he got into one of his rants.

"It's the weirdest thing," the teacher told me. "They don't say anything. They just stare at me."

"Well, that's their reaction to bullying," I said.

The teacher nodded. I don't think he realized I'd just called him a bully.

The children in the class were able to deal with him.

Most of the time, kids can deal with imperfection. Sometimes they can't, and then they need your help.

If our child is a different race from us, we should examine the diversity of the school. Sometimes there is a great deal of diversity; white children may be in the minority. Sometimes a school has few children of colour, and they are streamlined into low-expectation classes. If the students of colour are from a variety of races—Native, Asian, and black, for instance—it's less likely the teaching staff will show prejudicial attitudes than if there is a minority block of students from one cultural group. How will the student body's racial composition affect your child's social development and feeling of belonging? It is wise to assess this, as it likely will affect your child.

The elementary-school period is one of great activity, growth, and challenging behaviours. We see our child developing and work hard to influence that development. Other people influence our child, and we need to be alert and able to interpret, explain, and, if necessary, mitigate those influences. It is, as I remember it, a crazy-busy time.

Teens

I have over the course of the years interviewed fifty adopted teens. In the past, finding information on birth parents was a huge problem for them. With the advent of open adoption, more permissive government agencies, and the use of the Internet, it is less of a problem, but teens still have broken or no contacts with birth mothers. Or they have to contend with the issue of secrecy if they were adopted from a country that did not keep records or refused to release records. They may have to deal with birth families who deny contact or adoptive parents who refuse to allow contact with the birth family. It's not perfect out there. The underlying need of teens for information and contact with birth families is to help them establish their identity. Establishing identity is vital at this stage of their lives.

Creating an individual identity

From the parents' point of view, the teen's efforts to establish identity is fraught with emotions that can act as a roadblock to development in other parts of the teen's life. The problems of self-esteem, feelings of competence, academic and athletic achievements, and social development may be delayed as he tries to resolve his identity issues. It is as if he has to stop and wrestle with his identity before he can mature. Some teens find this task more difficult than others. As parents we find it hard to know when we should encourage separation and independent thinking and when we should clamp down and be controlling. After all, the teen who can carefully drive a two-ton truck through town is the same one who forgets to do his homework, leaves the oven on, and can't find his shoes. This may be the stage when teens can benefit from outside counselling, or at least make a plan on how to resolve their identity as an adopted member of the family. If they haven't made a plan to deal with this, parents can help them do so.

Part of establishing identity is recognizing one's sexual identity. Lesbian, gay, bisexual, and transgendered teens may find their sexual identity becomes clear to them at this time. Parents of adoptive teens have all the learning around identity issues of adopted teens to absorb along with those of LGBTQ teens. If our child tells us he or she is not heterosexual, and we do not understand her orientation, we could do with some advice. It is also wise to get information on state or provincial laws and social attitudes. Rather than deny that there is prejudice, examine it and be prepared for the prejudice the child might face. As well, look for contacts that reflect a positive view of the child. There are online groups and forums we can join. We can ask questions of our teens and listen to their answers. There are now groups for teens, often at school, where they can get advice, information, and acceptance. Our child is not only his sexual orientation, he is also a math student, a favourite grandchild, a musician, and many other composite parts. We can help him or her lead a balanced life.[13]

Planning for the future

I had an accountant once who told me, "If it works out on paper, it will work out in life." As a philosophy, this has a few flaws. Not everything is under our control; life happens; we can't always know what the future has in store, but planning does mean the future is *more likely* to happen as we expect.

This is not always obvious to teens who can live in the moment and think the future will look after itself, or are one of the lucky ones who will always succeed without effort or planning, or they are one of the unfortunates who will never succeed. It helps to encourage teens to make short-range plans. I'm a list-maker myself—but there are other ways. When the short-term plans come to fruition, encourage larger ones until your teen is used to looking a few years ahead and putting the steps in place to carry them out. We are working with an immature area of the adolescent brain here, the prefrontal cortex, where the ability to plan is not yet fully developed. If your family is used to using a white board or the door of the fridge, on which all the steps for an event such as a camping trip are set out and everyone's contributions added, teens can see the value of planning from an early age and will likely continue it. It's reassuring for parents to know their children are taking their own futures seriously.

Developing strong emotional bonds

The goal of parents is to help our children develop strong emotional bonds. Those bonds won't necessarily be only with us. We expect to keep their love, but in the teen years, they will establish bonds with others. We want to ensure those "others" are not the local mafia.

A strong emotional need for teens is to belong to a group. They may join sports teams, music bands, or game-playing online groups which can help them secure their identity. They may also join street gangs, religious cults, or other unsavoury groups. If they feel they don't belong in their school social group and aren't considered important or necessary, they will look outside it for affiliation. Parental love and affection are important, but emotional experience with others is important as well. Adopted children may have a push-pull dance with intimacy. They may expect every close relationship to end in abandonment. They may sabotage relationships, rejecting others before the other person can reject them. At an emotional level, they are trying to keep themselves safe from pain. Try to help them see that the breakup of a relationship is a chance to learn about the ways they look for closeness. Recognize that they tried to become intimate and help them with the pain of the separation.

The difficulty is they may not understand what is underneath their avoidance of intimate relations. They may feel anger or sorrow without knowing why they feel it. They may not be able to talk about it, but you, as a parent, can offer options on what they might be feeling: fear of rejection, sadness, lack of trust. It is hard to do, since teens often would rather talk to their friends than their parents, but persist—and offer to find a counsellor or mentor.

Developing confidence in problem-solving

This may not be difficult for your child. He may have had a great deal of experience in making decisions and solving problems. They develop their own style: My eldest made lists outlining the pros and cons; the second leaped into situations after having absorbed in some ethereal way what he needed to know and talked about it afterward; my youngest quietly listened to everyone, mentally weighed his pros and cons, and then acted. He didn't talk about it before or after.

They look to us to inspire them, show them our expectations, recognize their capabilities, and hold them responsible for their decisions.[14] This attitude shows we have faith in them. It's a fine line, though, between having faith and high expectations and putting too much pressure on them to be what we have decided they should be. We have to inspire—not drag them forward; show our expectations—not demand they choose a certain path; recognize their abilities without nagging and constant supervision. Listening to our teens sometimes requires superhuman ability. We are busy. They seem to take forever to come to the point. They can have wild ideas about how to solve a problem. A useful question when trying to listen to your teen is: What are your options? That allows the teen to explore all the ways in which he or she could solve the problem other than the reckless one that makes your hair stand on end. If we can stay with them through an exploration of the options, they often do decide on one we can live with.

We can, at this period in their lives, be attentive to opportunities that might be open to them. This may be when we find a same-race mentor, a professional in a field that might interest them, a counsellor, or an aunt or uncle who takes them on a trip. My sister, who was only eleven years older than my then fourteen-year-old son, asked if she could take him to a mediaeval tournament. There, adults dressed in costumes jousted and acted as if they were living in the fourteenth century. Of course I let him go. He had a wonderful time because, like my sister, he was into fantasy, games, and stories. Adults playing out roles suited him immensely. He met slightly odd but wonderful people and expanded his notion of "normal" behaviour. He was creative and artistic himself and felt right at home. My daughter, at age fifteen, asked if she could shadow a stockbroker for a day. She did that and decided it was not her career choice, but it expanded her world. We have friends and acquaintances who may be able to provide different experiences for our children. Helping them explore new worlds shows them we understand they are on the verge of adulthood and capable of planning.

Finding a place in society

This is all preparation to finding a secure place in society. This is the age we will likely share all the adoption information we have and help our child find more. If she has had an open adoption and knows her birth family, more information about them might be easy to find. If not, we can cooperate with her to find out as much as we can. She will integrate that information and create a place that feels comfortable. Our child may find herself slotted into society according to her race, and she may not feel comfortable there. She may need our help in finding some affiliations with people of her race and culture. We can help with this by taking a trip to our child's town of origin or the hospital where she was born. We may join more heritage gatherings at this time; attend music festivals that celebrate her heritage, such as Native pow wow dances. We need to keep in mind that our children are exploring a world different from ours while carrying a sense of loss and abandonment. Be prepared for their conflicting responses.

Offering support with limited control

Some advisors suggest that parents share power with their teens,[15] that we consult with them and discuss options and set limits, but make those limits broad. I can't quite imagine a calm, intellectual discussion of limits with a teen. It's usually a little more emotional—even wild. It's quite a dance. We have spent years setting limits, enforcing rules, discussing transgressions, establishing a sense of right and wrong in our children, and encouraging them to make good decisions, and suddenly they don't want us involved. We are lucky if they even speak to us, much less have a disinterested, calm planning session.

They are trying to find a way to be independent, but that doesn't mean they want us be indifferent. We must talk with them, negotiate, compromise at times, and try to reach agreement. With great effort, we can drag the discussion to calm, civil behaviour. This process models adult problem-solving behaviour. They learn it from us.

We are important; we do matter to them. It is sometimes difficult to see that. I understood, when my children were teens, they needed to find their own way and I needed to let most of my control over their lives detach bit by bit, but it was never clear to me exactly when it was appropriate or exactly how much control to let go. This is a time of messy trial and error. We have spent so much time and energy with them it feels strange not to be constantly involved. Teens still want to know parents are nearby, concerned, and ready to support them; at the same time, they are trying to be independent. When I interviewed thirty teens for my book on teen suicide prevention, I was shocked to find their parents were the most important influence in their lives—more important than their friends or love interest. If they had been able to talk to their parents, those teens told me, they would not have tried suicide. That was humbling and scary. If we are that important then we might surely get it wrong, and be responsible for a mess in their lives. Luckily, as they move into adulthood, teens are usually forgiving of us and our misguided efforts.

Psychologists have found that parents who use control methods such as threats to withdraw love, guilt-inducing comments, and other manipulative tactics produce children who are afraid to separate from their parents. Such parents sabotage their child's ability to make friends and develop intimate relationships.[16] It's another way to get it wrong.

Emotional blackmail might win the parents a short-term victory, but it will undermine their child's emotional development. Becoming independent is a goal of teenage life. Helping them to accomplish that while still maintaining supportive family ties is the parents' job.

Adopted teens who have not come to terms with their initial birth separation and trauma may be afraid to venture out into the world on their own and prefer to stay safely cocooned in the adoptive family. They are not going to risk rejection out there in the wild world of risky relationships. They will stick with what they know. Parents may not realize their child sets up a disruption in any promising relationship. They may not see a pattern until it has been established for many years. Their child begins a new relationship full of love and expectations of joy only to find fault and either leave the relationship or sabotage it so they are rejected. This is so common that when I meet someone who shows this pattern, I suspect they have unresolved adoption issues.

It is difficult to support our child's increasing need for independence while maintaining a close relationship. We can do it, but it sometimes is difficult to let them try out new personae, a new career choice, or a new set of friends. If our son's race is different from ours, it can be hard to watch him explore a culture in which we don't feel included. If we have friends from that culture or contact with groups from that culture, it is easier. We generally fear what we don't know, and becoming knowledgeable about his culture is reassuring during the teen years.

Teens are in the process of creating themselves. They are taking what we have offered and what they have inherited, and learning to forge their own identities. Giving them as much control over the process as we can is vital to that creation.

Young Adults

We aren't finished when they reach nineteen. Young adults still need their parents to act as a sounding board, a listening post, and a bank. The brain is still developing. The frontal lobe is the last to firm up its most used pathways and be a reliable processing centre. Young men take longer than women to do this and so may be making impulsive decisions well into their twenties while their brain pathways form.[17, 18]

The need for mentoring

Teens and young adults often learn best in a mentoring situation. When I have travelled to other countries, I have been impressed with the adult-youth working partnerships that seem to be part of other cultures. Other than our trade apprenticeship programs, our North American culture doesn't seem to offer many opportunities for young people to copy the work habits of adults, and so avoid risk-taking. A mentoring program may constrain the impetuous young, but it has some positive results. Young adults can take time to decide if the ways their mentors act is useful to them. They are competent. They have a great deal of brain development to work with—it's just not as efficient as it will become—and it takes a great deal of mental energy to coordinate what they do have to make decisions. They also get better as they age at noticing when their decisions are not wise. Following a mentor can give them practice at problem-solving while being guided away from disastrous decisions.

With or without a mentor, young adults still require parental guidance, although we may have to couch that guidance in diplomatic and cooperative terms.

What does independence look like?

Young adulthood is a difficult time for parents of adopted children. We want our children to be independent, make adult decisions, and find their own way in the world. We want them to develop separate and deep relationships with others while still remaining close to us emotionally. It is hard to know what kind of relationships with our children will best enhance their lives. It's hard to know if the fact that they don't call us for a month is a good thing or alarming. Should we offer to pay to get them out of difficulties or let them deal with the results of their own decisions? When we agree they can come home between jobs or between relationships, is that being warm and supportive or enabling irresponsible behaviour?

When I was a teenager, most people left home and went to work, so by their early twenties they had jobs, families, and usually a house and a mortgage. Now, such a secure environment is not possible for our children. There are few jobs that pay enough for them to move out. They may go to school well into their twenties and even into their thirties. They may marry later or not at all. They have children later or don't have children. It is difficult for parents to expect a predictable process. Knowing how to react so our children grow and develop in their twenties seems to be a "learn by doing" experiment.

We work hard during their early years to try to make them autonomous, independent problem solvers. It can be painful when they achieve that status and need us less and less. It seems to be a kind of abandonment to us; we are no longer the centre of their universe, knowing everything that goes on in their lives, influencing them and reaping the rewards of a close family. If they are independent, they likely don't want to discuss the minutiae of their day with us, ask our advice, or inform us of their every decision. It's a bit of a shock to realize our adult children are in charge of our relationship. We helped them to get to the position where they decide what the relationship will be. We must adjust and cooperate.

There are some books about this and some online forums that discuss this. It seems, though, the individual circumstances and needs of adult children—including financial stresses—play into the child-parent relationship in a much less predictable way than they do when the children are younger. It may be that young adults have not been studied as much as younger children and teens, but in this post-recession time, they face a unique set of challenges, including fewer job prospects, a widening rift between rich and poor and narrowing of the middle class, myriad career choices, and long post-secondary preparation periods, all factors that affect our children. They have been protected and may now feel entitled to our support. Parents can find it hard to see a "best practices" approach to the young adult stage.

We Still Love Them

We are committed to our children for their whole lives and may not be sure how to demonstrate our love when they are young adults. Adopted children might find it impossible to remove themselves very far from their adopted family, as they fear abandonment. Adoptive parents can face a difficult path, trying to give emotional support while encouraging independence. I still find it hard to know what action of mine is loving and what is interfering. I know I should talk less, listen more, and refrain from giving solutions as our children grow into adulthood, but it's hard to listen without offering to help. I still make mistakes there. Recently, my son called and laid out a problem he was having.

I said, "I'm really sorry, honey, but I can only pay for some of that."

His response was, "For God's sake, I'm not asking you for money. I'll figure it out."

My offer to help was insulting. I'm still learning to keep quiet. Luckily, he seems to be happy with a less than perfect mom.

They still need family, some more than others. We still need them in the family. We are not like spiders, raising offspring we drop out of the nest and never see again. We want to accept our children as part of the family with emerging and differing roles as they grow.

Keeping our relationships healthy takes work. Our children grow, change directions, gather new friends and lovers, establish their own families, and usually include us in the extended family cluster they create. We are still important. We just are less in control of their lives. We need to have faith that what we have offered and what we have created with them will sustain them and contribute to a full and rich life.

1   Brenda McCreight, "Attachment Disorder and the Adoptive Family." [No date.] https://davethomasfoundation.org/wp-content/uploads/2015/03/Attachment-pamphlet.pdf

2   Elizabeth Antunovic, "Kangaroo Mother Care: The Science of Skin-to-Skin Contact." *Boba* [No date.] http://www.boba.com/kangaroo-mother-care

3   Leighton-Hilborn and Lynda P. Haddon, "Preterm Birth: Kangaroo Care for Infants." Multiple Births Association of Canada, 2013. http://multiplebirthscanada.org/mbc_factsheets/FS_-_PTB-_Kangaroo_Care_23092014_Final.pdf

4   Jack Newman and Lenore Goldfarb, "Breastfeeding: The Protocols for Induced Lactation—A Guide for Maximising Breastmilk Production," *Asklenore.info*. [No date.] http://asklenore.info/breastfeeding/induced_lactation/adoptive_breast-feeding.shtml

5   Beth Hall and Gail Steinberg, *Inside Transracial Adoption: Strength-based, Culture-Sensitizing, Parenting Strategies for Inter-Country or Domestic Adoptive Families That Don't "Match"* (London and Philadelphia: Jessica Kingsley Publishers, 2013).

6   "Adoption at Different Ages: Adopting an Infant." Bethany Christian Services Lifelines Post-adoption Resources. [No date.] http://bethanylifelines.org/adoptees/adoption-at-different-ages/#infant

7   JoAnne Solchany, "12 Ways to Form a Healthy Attachment with Your Adopted Child." *Baby Center Expert Advice*, July 2014. http://www.babycenter.com/0_12-ways-to-form-a-healthy-attachment-with-your-adopted-child_1374194.bc

8   Child Welfare Information Gateway. *Impact of Adoption on Adoptive Parents* (Washington, DC: US Department of Health and Human Services, Children's Bureau, 2015). http://childwelfare.gov/pubs/factsheets/impact-parent/

9   "Horses for Courses: Why a Child's Position in the Family Influences Future Career Choices," *Childalert*. [No date.] http://childalert.co.uk/article.php?articles_id=330

10   Rachael Rettner, "Birth Order Affects Child's Intelligence and Personality." *Livescience*, August 12, 2010. http://livescience.com/6852-birth-order-affects-childs-intelligence-personality.html

11   David DiSalvo, "Despite Popular Assumptions, Birth Order Isn't Important, Says New Study." *Forbes*, July 22, 2015. http://forbes.com/sites/daviddisalvo/2015/07/20/despite-popular-assumptions-birth-order-isnt-important-says-new-study/

12   "Parenting Your Adopted School-aged Child: Fact Sheet for Families." Washington, DC: Child Welfare Information Gateway Children's Bureau, January 2015. http://childwelfare.gov/pubPDFs/parent-school-age.pdf

13   Luca Maurer, "Ten Tips for Parents of a Gay, Lesbian, Bisexual, or Transgender Child." *Advocates for Youth*. [No date.] http://advocatesforyouth.org/parents/173-parents

14   "A Research Update from Search Institute: Developmental Relationships." *Search Institute*, September 2014. http://search-institute.org/downloadable/Dev-Relationships-Framework-Sept2014.pdf

15   Ibid.

16   "Teens Whose Parents Exert More Psychological Control Have Trouble with Closeness, Independence," *EurekAlert*, October 23, 2014. http://eurekalert.org/pub_releases/2014-10/sfri-twp101614.php

17   Sara B. Johnson, Robert W. Blu, and Jay N. Giedd, "Adolescent Maturity and the Brain: The Promise and Pitfalls of Neuroscience Research in Adolescent Health Policy," *Journal of Adolescent Health* 45(3) (2009), 216-221. http://ncbi.nlm.nih.gov/pmc/articles/PMC2892678/

18   Molly Edmonds, "Are Teenage Brains Really Different from Adult Brains?" *HowStuffWorks*. [No date.] http://science.howstuffworks.com/life/inside-the-mind/human-brain/teenage-brain1.htm

7 The Changing World of Adoption

Types of Adoption

Adoptive parents and adoptees enter into adoption in three ways: as an open adoption, a closed adoption, or a mitigated adoption. They may find each other through various agencies, networks, or international organizations, but they all establish their relationship in one of these three ways.

Open adoption

The public view of adoption in North America has changed over the years. When we adopted our sons, few were open. Open adoptions were special cases: aunts or grandmothers adopted the child or step-parents adopted their partner's children. But the rest of us had little choice. Closed adoption was the only option offered. I always thought of my son's first mother on his birthday. I wished I could call her and let her know how he was doing; she must have wondered. I once tried to bluff my way into the courthouse records in my town. I got as far as having a clerk take me into the file room and reach for the file. She stopped and said, "Oh, it's closed. I can't let you see it." I was so near to finding the information, and it was so frustrating. I contemplated wrestling with her for it for a second but remembered the police were housed in the same building and restrained myself. Now open adoption is the norm.

Most domestic adoptions now (the child lives in the same country as the parents) are open; that is, there is full disclosure of information between the birth and adoptive families. Some continue to stay in touch. A report from 2012 found that two-thirds of private adoptions maintained contact between birth and adoptive families.[1] In open, full-disclosure adoptions, adoptive parents know the birth mother and sometimes the birth father. The birth parents' ideas and wishes are respected as much as possible. That's the goal, and some families put an amazing amount of effort into creating a co-operative agreement. It doesn't always go smoothly. Relatives are never uniformly wonderful. (Consider your own, and my point is clear.) Ongoing contact is usually worked out in some way, often with a contract, so both parties know the plan for the coming years. The purpose is to provide loving parents so the child feels he belongs firmly in his new family while knowing his family of origin. If he is lucky, he will be loved and supported by both. This should dispel the debilitating feelings of alienation of adopted teens when they don't know where they come from. It is an overwhelmingly difficult concept for most teens, as I found when I interviewed them.[2] Knowing your birth mother, whether she is amazing or really tedious, is much better than wondering if you are truly human and were dropped from a spaceship.

Ideally, open adoption should give a child a loving, adoptive family with connections to her birth family so she has affectionate birth grandparents, aunts, and uncles whom she visits occasionally while still firmly entrenched in her adoptive family. Since people are less than ideal, she may have an adoptive family who is fearful of the birth parents, who manipulate and restrict visits with that family, and who deprecate or even disparage them. Or she may have a birth family who is needy and drains the adoptive family of emotional and financial support. The birth plan contract may work out beautifully, but it may also fall to pieces. It's people who are making these contracts, and people can be unpredictable. We start with a good agreement and hope it works.

Once the adoptive family has completed the legal adoption process, the birth family has no more legal rights. If the adoption is disrupted, if the adoptive family neglect or repudiate the child, the birth family cannot swoop in and claim the child. Adoption is permanent. If the birth family has been involved over the years, they may be the logical ones to help if the relationship between the child and the adoptive parents disintegrates, but they do not have any legal right to do so. What birth families may feel is their right to parent is not a legal right.

Open adoption does not necessarily mean contact; it means both parties know each other. Greater or lesser contact is negotiated at the time of adoption. This is difficult timing because adoptive parents are likely to agree to whatever the birth parents ask in order to facilitate the placement, and birth parents may agree to what the adoptive parents ask in order not to jeopardize the placement. It can be mutually intimidating and not conducive to frank discussion.

In the days of closed adoption, adoptive parents were told when the baby was born and where to pick him or her up. My husband and I had little advance notice and no information ahead of time. When my eldest son was born, my husband was working in the bush, and I had to send a plane for him. He said the pilot fell asleep on the way back and he had to fly the small plane himself until the lake came into view. He woke up the pilot to land it. We packed up and drove eight hours to meet the social worker at the hospital. We knew very little about my son's birth parents, other than what was written in the history: his birth mother's age, the number of siblings, along with similar information for the birth father, who was a student at the local university. Both birth parents met with the social worker to plan the placement.

When our youngest son was born, we were living in the city, so we drove twenty minutes to visit him when he was four days old. It was also a closed adoption. The agency would not place either boy until they were ten days old because the birth mother, in those days, had ten days to change her mind. There was no thought of how the baby was coping with this. We didn't meet the birth mothers. We not only had little information from the social worker, some of it was wrong. It was not common to give adoptive parents a report of more than a page or two, highly redacted. In both cases we didn't know anything about the birth family until the baby had been born and placed with us. There was no advanced arrangement, no getting to know each other.

In open adoption, adoptive parents can be very involved with the pregnancy and birth, even paying for the care of the birth mother (in the US). They can meet the birth relatives, be involved in decision making, and contribute to the birth as much as possible. They can even attend the birth. And the birth mother can still change her mind. Some adoptive parents go through this process three or four times. It must be heartbreaking. When it goes smoothly, it can be thrilling. The adoptive family is involved early, the birth family respects the boundaries the adoptive family requests, and the child feels loved and supported by all. The adoptive parents feel satisfied that all is well.[3] Open adoption works beneficially for adoptive parents some of the time. It is the best option for adoptees most of the time. Studies indicate that a greater openness results in greater satisfaction for adoptive parents, birth parents, and adoptees.[4] But people are not perfect, and we deal with what we get.

Closed adoptions were far from perfect. We need more data

on the results, but we can expect that children of open adoptions will have an easier time in their teen and young adult years than children of closed adoption as they will have worked out their identity with solid information. They will be unlikely to fantasize about the rich birth father or glamorous birth mother they never knew. I expect they will see themselves as a real person with real ancestors who grew up with real adoptive parents. They will still need to deal with loss and the sense that they were somehow not acceptable to their birth parents, but they will have a better chance of asking those questions and reconciling to the answers than they would have in the past.

Mitigated or facilitated adoption

In mitigated or facilitated adoption, the adoptive parents and birth parents usually do not know each other but communicate through an agent or lawyer. Some contact after birth is maintained this way; birth parents can ask for reports on their child, and adoptive parents can offer information and updates and ask questions of the birth parents through the facilitator. This process has the advantage of providing a source of information to the adoptee in the teen years, if the birth parents keep in touch with the agency or lawyer. There will be agents who have integrity, and there will be some who have a strong profit motive and lack integrity. The efficacy of the process may depend on the integrity of the facilitator. Facilitators are generally unlicenced and have no regulatory body governing them. The may not practice legally in all areas. While I know they exist, I haven't met one. I assume the facilitator creates a contractual agreement between the birth family and the adoptive family in a business-like process. They avoid face-to-face contact with a social worker or birth parent and offer no professional counselling or home visits.

Mitigated adoptions are no doubt less emotional than open adoptions. Our North American society still has strong pockets of culture that distrust emotion.

Closed or confidential adoptions

While domestic adoptions for newborns are most often open, some people want closed or confidential adoptions. Such adoptive parents do not want any interaction with or interference from birth families, or they fear birth families are so dysfunctional they will be harmful to the child—which, on occasion, may be correct. Adoptive parents may feel they can deal with the problems of teens and young adults who want information about their birth families, or they decide they will look for information at a later time. I know I feared that if his birth mother saw what a wonderful, adorable, delightful child my son was, she'd surely want him back, and that would have squeezed my heart in unbearable pain. When the adoptions were final—at one year for my eldest son and at three years for my youngest—I was more comfortable and would have welcomed contact. Open adoption may force adoptive parents to face those fears more realistically than I did.

Some birth mothers may feel that their child needs protection from their own parents or siblings and will ask for a closed adoption. They may want to put closure on this episode of their life and avoid having to make explanations about the child to their own family members. It is helpful if they can provide as much information about themselves and the birth father as possible. Medical information given at the time of birth usually reports only good health since the mother is young, her parents are relatively young, and some family diseases have not yet developed. Contact information lodged with the agency can provide the means for birth and adoptive parents to share ongoing information and requests. The adoption agency can forward such information as medical updates or questions about medical history both ways as the child matures. I wish this happened routinely. It's possible, but unlikely.

International or intercountry adoptions are often closed because records are not available or because it is the practice in the child's country of origin. The Hague Convention on Intercountry Adoption, 1993,[5] requires adoption agencies preserve information about the child. Agencies in countries that were signatories to the convention should have background information on each child who is adopted. The convention was put in place to counteract child trafficking and profiteering by adoption agencies. While international adoption may take longer now as countries ratify and implement the Hague Convention, adoptive parents can be more assured that the process is honest and legal.

The number of international adoptions has slowed over the last few years. In Canada, it declined fifty-six percent from 2010 to 2014 and, in the US, it dropped seventy percent.[6] There appear to be just as many people inquiring about international adoption, but the combination of the tightening of the process through adherence to the Hague Convention and the restrictions placed on adoption in some countries have reduced the number of children available. It is amazing how quickly the sources of adoptable children change. A legislative decree can come suddenly and sometimes even affect adoptive parents as they are packing up in a foreign hotel, hours away from taking their baby home. A decree can make the adoption process suddenly impossible.

Adoptive parents must use an agency in international adoptions, a lawyer, and immigration authorities. The paperwork can take over your house. Permissions necessary to bring your child home can vary from province to province and state to state. In some areas you can apply for your child's citizenship when you bring him home, but in others you must sponsor your child as an immigrant.[7] It isn't simple, but it is possible. The forms listed on the US government site are impressively detailed.[8] I am always struck by the American use of the word "alien." I imagine the child coming from Mars via spaceship. Canadian forms refer to the child as "your adopted child."[9] The paperwork is onerous, but applying domestically also requires a mountain of it. Adoptive parents must become inured to it. Because the process takes some time, internationally adopted children are usually over six months of age when placed and can be much older. As in domestic adoptions, there are Internet sites where you can see the children who are available and from what countries. Adoption agencies can provide photos, and you can scan the sites of the many children waiting for homes.

The enforcement of the strict Hague Convention rules has meant the process of adopting is more expensive than it was and more difficult to maneuver. Agencies are closing their doors, leaving prospective parents out money, time, and emotional investment. Some countries have increased their restrictions on adoptive parents. China will not take applications from prospective parents who are same-sex, obese, have alcoholic parents or cancer in the family.[10] It must have been a fascinating boardroom collection of bigots when they came up with that list.

Embryo adoption/donation

It is not possible to adopt an embryo; we can only adopt a child. Presently, embryos are considered property, and ownership of the embryo is contracted between the donor or donor agency and the recipients. The states of Georgia and Louisiana have slightly different laws, but they also do not consider the embryo a child. In the US and Canada, the woman who has been implanted with an embryo is considered the legal mother of the child, and her legal spouse is considered the other parent.[11] Morality and technology have combined to create laws that are at least as reasonable and practical as can be managed. Embryos can be donated by couples who have frozen embryos for in-vitro fertilization (IVF) and who have no further need of those stored embryos. There seems to be no definitive best-before-use or past-prime date for the embryos. One woman used an embryo that had been stored for nineteen years and had a healthy baby.[12] (There must be an apocalyptic movie plot somewhere about a freezer full of embryos populating the new planet.) Today, many families are eternally grateful for the process. The possibilities of implanting embryos in women who need them or in surrogate mothers who grow the child for an adoptive parent are multiplying faster than ethicists can keep up and faster than legislation can adjust.

While an embryo is not a legal person, agencies may treat this embryo donation contract as an adoption and require the same kind of checks into the recipients' emotional, financial, and physical stability as they would for a child placement. This seems reasonable since it is going to result in a child. Agencies may provide the prospective parents with descriptions of the egg and sperm donors and offer counselling around the transaction. They also may use the term "adoption" when discussing the donation. Not all agencies or clinics do so. One Canadian clinic stores embryos, and when a donor wishes to relinquish them, the first person on the waiting list is offered an embryo. There is no matching, although the clinic does assess both sets of parents for psychosocial problems.[13]

While donors are not allowed by law to receive payment for their embryo, clinics in both countries can charge the recipients fees for their services. Agencies can give advice on the contract the receiving parents make with the donor. Some genetic parents may wish for further contact and may want to take some responsibility for the child's future. This needs to be made clear when the contract is written. Establishing trust between the donor and recipients is important because neither they nor the child can rely on legislation. There is no legislation in either the US or Canada that governs embryo donation other than contract law. The children have no legal recourse to information or contact with their genetic parents. The genetic parents, once they sign the contract, have no legal rights to information about the resulting child, so this initial contract is crucial.

Embryo recipients will likely face the same questions from their teens that adoptive parents do: What is my genetic background? Who do I look like? Where in the universe is my biological family? Where do I belong? Because that is likely, donating parents need to consider the identity concerns of adoptees as pertinent to their embryo-donated child. Are they prepared for a teen to pop around to their house fifteen years after the donation to see what they look like?

Embryo donation seems a cost-effective way to have a baby. It is much cheaper than IVF and has a much higher success rate.[14] Recipients can feel more in control of the situation, and can have their babies more quickly than through IVF or adoption. They are assured of having a newborn and have been responsible for the care and feeding of the baby in utero. This reassures many parents that their baby will not suffer the effects of poor nutrition or drugs while in utero. The mother is able to go through the pregnancy process, as some mothers fervently wish. I thought once was enough myself and didn't miss it a bit when I adopted, but others feel differently. The implanted baby is "born to," but she is not "born of."

Adoption starts to look simple when we look at the ethics and moral concerns of embryo donation. While the donated embryo baby is "born to" the recipients, she does not have their biology, so she can look much different from the rest of the family. She will likely not have the abandonment issues of adopted children—although we don't have studies on that yet. It seems reasonable that the child would not suffer separation trauma as she spent nine months *in vivo* with her birth mother. She may have talents and proclivities that are different from her adoptive family. Not all families accept differences well. While some parents can choose the donors, others cannot, and a surprise difference in race can be a challenge. No one told them that great grandfather Matthew in the donor's family was not of their race. Donor parents can feel as though they have given up a baby and owe the child an explanation of why he or she was "given away." Donor parents worry that if embryos are disbursed by a clinic with no adoption-like process, then many children in a small geographical area could turn out to be related to one another. Quite a possibility. Do their teens need a DNA test for every partner they date? After all, that cute girl he feels an affinity for might be his sister. The process for embryo donation seems a little careless.

Changes in Who Adopts

Creating a modern family is, for the most part, a conscious decision. With efficient birth control and abortion services, few people need to have a baby unless they want one. Adoption has always been a conscious decision, but now it shares that purposeful nature with those who birth a baby. In some ways adoption has become simply another way to have a child not so different from the biological process.

Adoptive families are well above the poverty line. Our children receive attention: they are read to, taken to hockey, karate, and ballet, and are generally involved in more organized activities than biological children.[15] Since surveys deal with general trends, they will include celebrity parents who can certainly skew income averages out of any realistic boundaries, balancing those of us who blunder along managing to keep the insurance premiums up and the mortgage paid. No doubt we who adopt are much like most people who simply want a family—ordinary people doing ordinary things one day at a time. Adoption agencies now encourage single women and single men, same-sex couples, and older couples to adopt—at least many agencies do. So adoptive parents are more varied than they used to be. Children are more varied as well. Trends show differences in children's racial composition and age at adoption because adoptive parents must respond to political decisions around who can adopt in which country, to natural disasters that leave children destitute and orphaned, and to our ongoing child welfare systems, which promote certain sectors of adoptable children.

Foster parent adoptions

I was surprised to find the majority of adoptions are from foster care. In the US, thirty-seven percent of adopted children were adopted from foster care (2013 statistics).[16] From 2007 to 2013, international and private adoptions decreased[17] while the foster care adoptions increased. Agencies encourage foster parents to consider adoption and facilitate the process, whereas in the past they discouraged it. A marketing push by adoption organizations in North America promotes "permanency" instead of "placement," making it possible to look at many types of families, including foster families. The "heart galleries" (travelling exhibits that display photos and audiovisuals of foster children up for adoption) and marketing pages of adoption agencies put forth adoptable children from foster care in an attractive way, showing them living with foster families and therefore appearing socially competent and "just like us." Agency representatives take videos and photo banners depicting adoptable children to different areas of the community and display them to people who may consider adopting from foster care. For middle-class families, adoption from foster care is the most affordable option. It has the advantage of giving the adoptive parents a great deal of information about the child while giving the child, depending on age, the chance to learn about the adoptive parents and be part of the adoption decision.

Changing Role of Agencies

With changes in social attitudes, disasters throughout the world that create orphans, and fluctuating government financial support, the roles of helping agencies also change.

Government agencies

Government adoption agencies have moved from a somewhat calculated system of assigning a child to a family matched through written reports to a more involved process in which adoptive parents are given education, support, and a more co-operative role in the placing of the child. The birth mother is also given more control over the placement of her child, and as is common, the process is open, and both sets of parents, under the auspices of the adoption agency, meet to create a birth plan. That's the theory, anyway, and what we hope happens. As in all human endeavours, the efficacy of the process depends on the goodwill of the participants. Well-intentioned and competent agency workers, adoptive parents, and birth parents should be able to make a stable and secure plan for the child. Adoption workers in government offices are now educated around adoption issues such as separation trauma and can serve adoptive parents, birth parents, and adoptees with their expertise. They still face the pressure of having many more children, particularly older and special-needs children, to place than homes to place them in,[18] and in some areas are vastly overworked. We still expect excellence from them.

Government agencies usually set the standards of practice and influence legislation. They must respond to legislation and carry out the laws. They can get enmeshed in the rules. I overheard a social worker responding to a young adult's complaint that once her social worker left her with a different worker, she never heard from her again. "And she was my friend, or so I thought," the young woman said. The social worker responded, "But those are the rules. After a child is assigned a different social worker, the first one can't contact her." It was as if the rules were more important than the foster child's need for contact. I've worked for the government. A little healthy rebellion in the name of compassion and fairness is often possible. In fact, I believe it is the role of government agents to be the first to make changes.

Private and religious agencies

Private agencies usually model themselves after government agencies in providing education and ongoing support to adoptive parents. Since they are acting as your agent, they should be working for you. Some adoptive parents find paying an agency gives them a feeling of control over the process. Private agencies must be licenced, which means they should be regulated. In Canada, provincial laws govern the licensing of agencies; in the US, state law governs them. To assess the credibility and reliability of an agency in the US, check with the State Attorney General's department to find out if there are any lawsuits against that agency. I did not see a comparable service in Canada but assume the provincial ministry supervising placements would be a good place to start. Get the names of some adoptive parents this agency has served (if they can give you those) and talk to the parents. Schmooze with adoptive parents in a local parenting group, asking about the agency.[19]

Religion-based agencies are private and subject to the same scrutiny and regulation as other private agencies. I know they should be above reproach, but some are not. Check them out. You may find they suit you very well if you are part of that faith-based group and feel comfortable working with them. Before you adopt, compare the adoption education they provide and the ongoing support they offer with the services offered by public or other private agencies. Faith-based agencies are supported by a particular religious community and usually want to place children from relinquishing birth mothers of their community into their particular religious group.

Private agencies have been active, sometimes honestly and sometimes not, in international adoptions. With the introduction of the Hague Convention rules and with the ban on adoption from countries such as Russia, some agencies have closed their doors. This left some adoptive parents without a child and thousands of dollars poorer. Like any other business, private adoption agencies can find it unprofitable to continue. It seems cynical to be on the lookout for charlatans and profit-seeking business people in the adoption world, but they are there. It saddens me because I remember when some lawyers in my community did adoptions for no payment, just charging the registration fees, as a gracious contribution to the adoptive parents' happiness. It should be about happiness and love, but there are some who see children as a business commodity, slipping dangerously close to child trafficking.

Adopting children costs money. Where there is a lot of money, there are opportunists who seek to profit, and the adoption industry is no exception. Unscrupulous people set up adoption agencies that round up children in lands where poverty and lack of education make parents vulnerable to advances by agency representatives. Some birth parents are tricked into thinking they are temporarily giving their child to a benevolent family, while they remain the parents of the child.

Such agencies took advantage of natural disasters such as the 2010 earthquake in Haiti and desperate times in the countries they targeted. Scandals emerged. In December 2010, the government of Ethiopia revoked the licence of Better Future Adoption Services, a US agency, and accused them of trafficking in children and falsifying documents. Apparently most of the children, whom the agency described as orphans, were not. The adoptive parents, who had accepted "orphans," now had those children in their homes and had bonded with them as their sons or daughters. They had to face the fact that the agency had left a grieving family on the other side of the world. The agency's defence was that since it was faith-based, it couldn't do anything wrong.[20]

The escapades of Laura Silsby, who was caught trying to abduct and transport children from Haiti[21] and charged with criminal association and kidnapping, brought attention to the illegal and detrimental practices of some adoption agencies that removed children from other countries. Although Silsby's charges were eventually reduced from conspiracy and child abduction to "arranging irregular travel," she was convicted and served time in jail. All the children she tried to remove from Haiti had a parent. Her "rescue" of these children was illegal. But buoyed by her sense of righteousness, she thought she was justified as she had a Christian zeal for "rescuing, loving and caring for orphaned, abandoned, and impoverished Haitian and Dominican children"[22]—a laudable motive, but an unscrupulous practice.

Several agencies, such as God's Littlest Angels, the Zoe Foundation, and the Vision Forum Ministries, complained about the regulations and oversights that the United Nations Children's Fund (UNICEF) demanded.[23] Not every evangelical ministry objected to oversight, regulation, and honest accounting of a child's history. Many insisted on re-evaluating both the philosophy and practice of out-of-country adoption, as one would expect reasonable people to do. The exposure of Christian agencies that swept into countries and removed children illegally and immorally from their country and family of origin has thoroughly horrified many in the faith communities.

Out-of-country adoptions still proceed. Children still need homes, and adoptive parents still need children. However, adoptive parents now proceed with more caution and less trust that all faith-based agencies are necessarily moral.

Role of the birth mother in placement

The birth mother's role has changed a great deal over the past few years. Birth mothers aren't as easily intimidated as they used to be. They can be aggressive about finding exactly what they want for their child, socially supported in making that choice, and are likely to want an open adoption. Social workers generally encourage their participation in the birth plan. A birth mother's request for open adoption is usually honoured.

Some birth mothers want ongoing contact and some even a "favourite aunt" status. Others may not want continuing contact, just to be informed of their child's welfare. Others may demand a closed adoption. Despite counselling to the contrary, if a birth mother wants a closed adoption, it will likely occur. Because there are fewer babies than families who want them now, birth mothers of newborns can dictate much of the birth plan.

Culturally aware families

This is much more important today than it was seen to be in the past. Adoptive parents now must plan to integrate their child into her culture. In the past, many adoptive parents tried to do this, but there was no expectation that they *would* do so. Now there is. Adoptive parents need to make a plan to find a cultural group that will accept their child and where she will be comfortable. They must work to help her make her place in it. Since most of us aren't sociologists, ethnologists, or psychologists, this can be a mammoth demand. Luckily, there is support and help from various culture-specific groups to give us advice and encouragement.

What happens to adoptees' sense of place and identity when they get older? I find that when the child accepts a place in his cultural group, we do not lose our child to the culture; we gain a small place outside the culture as an ally. We can be aware of the way in which culture affects our child; we cannot share it, but we can stay close and support them. The members of his culture can also support and encourage him. It does work. It is sometimes uncomfortable, but that says more about the adoptive parents' need to adjust than the wisdom of acculturalization. I have been lucky in that my son's Aboriginal culture is a polite and respectful one where I have been met with courtesy. My culture (Scottish) values independence, but when I attend an Aboriginal feast I do not get my own food. I am an elder there. I sit with the older women and wait for some bright-eyed young child to bring me food. Charging around in my usual self-propelled manner will not do and would embarrass my son. We can learn.

LGBTQ families

Placement of children in LGBTQ families is more likely now than in the past, although there are some private agencies, predominantly fundamentalist religious ones, that do not accept adoptive parents from this group (and entire countries like China that legislate against it). Generally, though, the rest of society is much more accepting and receptive. Support and advice comes from both the LGBTQ communities and adoption agencies. Society is slowly changing.

In the last twenty years, a number of children's book authors battled prejudice—some people radically opposed the notion that LGBTQ people are part of society—to have their books, depicting same-sex parents, accepted into libraries. Things have changed. It isn't all peace and support out there, but we are getting more egalitarian. While there is still prejudice, there is much more acceptance than in the past, and adoption is now seen as the way in which many LGBTQ couples can create a family.

Emotional Effects of Adoption

We finally understand some of the effect adoption has on adoptees. The post-traumatic stress disorder research on adoptees helps us to understand that most do suffer emotional repercussions from being separated from their birth mothers. The operative word here is "emotional." North Americans are not always well-educated in emotions, and it takes time and counselling to understand that emotions matter.

Some of this understanding comes from the research around the effects of adoption that we read, discuss, and come to accept; this influences adoption policy. Some improvements have come about because adoption activists were determined that adoptive parents understand the nature of separation trauma. Whatever the reason, we have moved to a new understanding of adoption and its effect on our adopted children. Advice is available from agencies, adoptive family associations, and on the Internet in blogs and forums, so we can continue to learn and question our reactions, our child's reactions, our plans, and our expectations. It's a challenge, but it is more possible to raise an emotionally healthy child today than it was even ten years ago. Looking back, I'm horrified by some of the things I said to my children—because I didn't know any better.

Influence of Celebrity Adoptions

Celebrities seem to be glamorized models of personhood, a tantalizing glimpse of what we might have been if circumstances had been different. They are our fairy-tale fantasies who replace those princes and princesses from our childhood books and movies. Celebrities live in a far-away glittering world of charm and luxury. We can realize that they are on their third divorce, have trouble with crack cocaine, and are not necessarily kind without giving up on our belief in their beautiful lives. It's amazing how humans can hold contradictions without much mental discomfort. We look for glimpses of the ordinary in their perfect lives and some of us try to relate to them as ordinary people in spite of their lifestyle. Adoption may be one place where we share some of their lives.

Brad Pitt and Angelina Jolie, Madonna, and other celebrities have adopted children, some transracially from Africa. A report from the Africa Child Policy Forum indicates that many are following their example.[24] While most would agree that developing countries need to put energy and money into providing for orphaned children and supporting families so that children can remain at home, many children from poverty-stricken countries still need homes. It is hard to condemn anyone, celebrity or common workers like the rest of us, for offering a home to a child. Nor should we condemn the influence such celebrities have in directing adoptive parents to the need in Africa, although many critics have complained that celebrities adopt children like accessories—fourteen new pairs of shoes, another house in Hawaii, and two more kids. I don't see it that way. I'll confess that I am ignorant of the minutiae of the lives of the rich and famous, but in my view those celebrities seem to be trying hard to be good parents. If we set aside the value of nannies, chauffeurs, ski trips, and huge houses, they are muddling through the adoption process like the rest of us.

Why as North Americans are we influenced by celebrities? Adoption statistics show more interest in adoption from Africa when celebrities adopt from there. The marketing stats tell us that celebrities appear to influence around twenty-seven percent of eighteen- to-thirty-six-year-olds to support causes, although they influence fewer older Americans.[25] For psychological reasons beyond me, we do, or at least some of us do, respond to celebrities. While celebrity adoptions can spark an interest in adoption, the practical path takes time and effort, so adoptive parents need to be committed for the long term and have a sustaining interest in adoption in order to add to their family in this way. Celebrities may have inspired adoptive parents, but they will not stand by them; parents need to look to their own circle of family and friends and adoption association group to help them struggle through the angst of midnight fevers, the slog of math homework, and the gong show of adolescence.

Trending toward Love

Wherever the trend in adoption is going, it is going to be grounded in love. A willingness to work out a birth plan with all concerned parties—birth parents, step-parents, the owners of a donor embryo who may feel like birth parents, relatives, older adoptees, and adoptive parents—all can be united in a loving purpose. The agents who work for children are often fired by love and compassion to do their very best for the children in their care. The foster parents who are determined that the child in their care will feel safe and loved are part of the future of adoption. Love is a large part of this process.

We have progressed from a culture that saw children as property to one where they are valued individuals. In the future, adoptive parents may be accepted or rejected depending on the amount of love they can offer a child. And who knows? With the advances in quantum physics, we may be able to measure that.

1   Deborah H. Siegel and Susan Livingston Smith, *Openness in Adoption: From Secrecy and Stigma to Knowledge and Connections* (New York: Evan B. Donaldson Adoption Institute, 2012.) http://adoptioninstitute.org/old/publications/2012_03_OpennessInAdoption.pdf

2   Marion Crook, *The Face in the Mirror: Teens and Adoption* (Vancouver: Arsenal Pulp Press, 2000).

3   Xiaojia Ge, et al, "Bridging the Divide: Openness in Adoption and Post-adoption Psychosocial Adjustment among Birth and Adoptive Parents," *Journal of Family Psychology* 22(4), 2008: 529–540. http://www.ncbi.nlm.nih.gov/pmc/articles/PMC2638763/

4   Siegel and Livingston Smith, *Openness in Adoption*.

5   HCCH Hague Conference on Private International Law. http://hcch.net/index_en.php?act=text.display&tid=45

6   Isabelle Khoo, "International Adoption Rates Plummet In Canada," *Huffington Post Canada*, May 7, 2015. http://huffingtonpost.ca/2015/05/07/international-adoption_n_7225150.html

7   "Adopt a Child from Abroad." Government of Canada. [No date.] http://cic.gc.ca/english/immigrate/adoption/index.asp

8   "Intercountry Adoption: Forms." Bureau of Consular Affairs, US Department of State. [No date.] http://travel.state.gov/content/adoptionsabroad/en/adoption-process/forms.html

9   "Apply—Immigration Process." Government of Canada, October 23, 2012. http:// cic.gc.ca/english/immigrate/adoption/apply-how.asp

10 Tralee Pearce, "The Painful New Realities of International Adoption." *Globe and Mail*, February 17, 2012. http:// theglobeandmail.com/life/parenting/the-painful-new-realities-of-international-adoption/article547159/?page=all

11 "Adopter FAQs." Embryo Adoption Awareness Center. [No date.] http://embryo-adoption.org/adopters/adopting_parent_faq.cfm

12 Sarah Elizabeth Richards, "Get Used to Embryo Adoption," *Time*, August 24, 2013. http://ideas.time.com/2013/08/24/get-used-to-embryo-adoption/

13 Angela Krueger, "An Overview of Embryo Donation in Canada." *FertilityMatters. ca*. [No date.] http://iaac.ca/en/584-269-an-overview-of-embryo-donation-in-canada-by-angela-krueger-spring-2011-5

14 Rebecca Buckwater-Poza, "The Frozen Children: The Rise—and Complications—of Embryo Adoption in the U.S.," *Pacific Standard*, May 5, 2014. http://psmag.com/politics-and-law/frozen-children-rise-complications-embryo-adoption-u-s-80754

15 "Adopted Children," *Child Trends Data Bank*, August 2012. http://childtrends.org/?indicators=adopted-children

16 Cathy Payne, "Adoption Numbers Rising for Kids in Foster Care," *USA Today*, August 12, 2013. http://usatoday.com/story/news/nation/2013/08/12/adoption-foster-care/2643505/

17 "National Foster Care Adoption Attitude Survey: 2013 Executive Summary & Detailed Findings." Dave Thomas Foundation For Adoption, 2013. https://dciw4f53l7k9i.cloudfront.net/wp-content/uploads/2013/07/DTFA-HarrisPoll-REPORT-USA-FINALl.pdf

18 "Adoption Trends," *Infoplease*. [No date.] http://infoplease.com/us/statistics/adoption-trends.html

19 "How to Assess the Reputation of Licensed, Private Adoption Agencies," Washington, DC: Child Welfare Information Gateway, Children's Bureau, 2004. https://www.childwelfare.gov/pubs/twenty/

20 Kathryn Joyce, "'The Child Catchers': Evangelicals and the Fake-Orphan Racket," *The Daily Beast*, April 23, 2013. http://www.thedailybeast.com/witw/articles/2013/04/24/kathryn-joyce-s-the-child-catchers-inside-the-shadowy-world-of-adoption-trafficking.html

21 "Haiti Charges Baptists with Kidnapping Children," CBC News, February 4, 2010. http://www.cbc.ca/news/world/haiti-charges-baptists-with-kidnapping-childen-1.870826

22 Ginger Thompson, "Case Stokes Haiti's Fear for Children, and Itself," *The New York Times*, February 1, 2010. http://www.nytimes.com/2010/02/02/world/americas/02orphans.html?pagewanted=all

23   Matthew Bigg, "Haiti Orphans at Risk from Traffickers, Government, UNICEF," Reuters, January 25, 2010. http://www.reuters.com/article/us-quake-haiti-orphans-sb-idUSTRE60O2A120100125

24   Jacey Fortin, "Adopting from Africa: The Complicated Truth Behind a Celebrity Fad," *International Business Times*, May 30, 2012. http://ibtimes.com/adopting-africa-complicated-truth-behind-celebrity-fad-705521

25   "How Influential Are Celebrities?" *Watershed Publishing*, updated February 7, 2014. http://www.marketingcharts.com/television/are-celebrities-that-influential-38018/

8 Search and Reunion

Finding birth parents is no problem for adoptees in an open adoption. They already know who their first parents are. No search is required. It can be difficult when the adoption is closed. Information on the birth family can be unavailable, destroyed, or hidden. The adoptee usually can search through registry channels at the age of majority, and in some jurisdictions before that with the adopted parents' permission, but often when adoptive parents try to search they hit closed files that prevent any enlightenment.

Adoptees have common motives for searching for birth parents, particularly birth mothers. They want to know their original name and their "tribal affiliations," the people who are most like them and who may look like them. They need to establish contact with their birth mothers or families to elicit a sense of belonging. They often want to increase their affinity to their culture. And many want medical information.

Before the Search Begins

Each adoptive parent must work out their own path to reunion. There are a few steps to reunion that most groups advise: prepare for emotional upheaval; take it easy; get support; and deal with the outcome. Before the search begins, consider how your child's first parents will fit into your family. What does your child want? What do you want? And can you negotiate these wants and needs? It's a challenge.

Be prepared

If you work in the field of public health and social issues, you may have many colleagues who will listen and support you through search and reunion. Best friends can listen. Relatives can advise. Much better is finding a support group of adoptive parents affiliated with an adoptive family association, which provides professional staff and the latest information.

It helps to read the blogs that pepper the Internet to hear first-hand how emotionally charged a reunion is. Tears are part of the event. When you factor in that many reunions occur when the adoptee is in his or her late teens—a time when our children do not necessarily have experience in handling the extremes of emotions—we know it will be difficult. As well, we may not be experts in emotions ourselves. We might not recognize what we feel until it whacks us over the head.

We may want fervently to support our child's search and reunion, but it may be painful for us. We want our children to have that connection to their birth families because, in the long run, we know it will be better for them, and we want whatever is best for them. If we are not supportive, our children simply won't tell us they are searching, and then they'll suffer all the guilt and fear of hurting us that goes with that secrecy. The teens I interviewed told me that the compulsion to find their birth family was so strong some searched regardless of the objections of their adoptive parents. Some don't search while they are still living at home but wait until they move out.

Birth families are not always welcoming. After years of searching, one of my young friends discovered her birth mother and siblings only to find that her birth mother did not want to see her. Her birth mother spoke to her on the phone and gave her the name of her father. Subsequent DNA testing showed either the birth mother did not know who the father was or she lied. That was a second disappointment. Her birth mother told her not to contact her siblings, but since her siblings were in their late teens and early twenties, my young friend ignored that request and contacted them. She got some information and some sense of belonging from them. We speculated about why her birth mother wouldn't allow contact. My friend thought she may have been a result of incest. When you don't have the facts, you examine all the possibilities. Perhaps the circumstances of my friend's birth were so painful her birth mother could not bring them up again, and facing her child would mean she would have to face the pain of the past. My friend said she was better for having looked and found her family, because however unsatisfactory the connection was, at least she knew them.

Ask yourself ...

+ Is the reunion possible?
+ What part of it is possible?
+ What does your child want to do to make it possible?
+ What does he or she want you to do to assist?
+ How will your child's first parents fit into your family?
+ What does your child want?
+ What do you want?
+ Can you negotiate this?

Your child's emotional readiness

The stories of others revealed in online blogs can inform our thinking about reunions. We may have a reasonable expectation, a vision in our minds, of what a reunion will be like for our child, but the experiences of others can expose more possibilities. We need to be prepared and simply have faith our child will react with the skills she has developed and will confide in us or her support network when she needs us. It is a confounding and profound notion that we cannot live our child's life, cannot control it, and we have to give her room to make choices while staying close enough to support her as necessary. It's not easy.

What does your child want? Specifically? Generally? Usually, a child will begin with a specific motivation: "I want to know if I look like her," or, "I just want to know why." The first request will be easy to satisfy in a reunion; the second will be much harder, but both are examples of a specific reason for searching. With more discussion and more time for your child to think, she will often realize she has more questions and more reasons. Those will be personal, but they may also follow some general themes shared by adoptees: to know they had a beginning in a specific family; to find a place in that family; and to satisfy identity concerns about place in family, society, and race. They may also look for a way to extend their family and find more people to love and be loved by, especially if that love is lacking in their adoptive family.

Emotional readiness may be hard to judge. A child, especially a teen, may not want to reveal the extent of her yearning for fear of hurting us, her adoptive parents. Some teens simply don't talk about emotions or talk very little about how they feel. We may need to offer search and reunion options often enough so our child believes we do want to help and that searching is both possible and expected.

Rejection after a reunion will feel like rejection for a second time—the first when "given away" for adoption and the second when the birth mother meets her child and again turns away. This is very, very hard to take.

Reunion counselling

Start locally. What is available in a face-to-face community and what is available online? Get counselling from an experienced therapist or advisor who knows the complicated world of reunions.

Your emotional readiness for reunion

There is a bucket-load of information on the emotional turmoil of reunion for adoptees and birth mothers. I haven't found anything on the feelings that flood adoptive parents. I expect our greatest fear is that our child will be hurt—and they might be—or that our child will experience wild swings of emotions we don't expect or know how to cope with—and that can happen as well.

One site described the first contact as a "delicate process." That is, perhaps, a massive understatement. Emotions will not only surface, they may erupt like an undersea explosion and surge through our life. Not always and not necessarily, but reunions can be difficult. Reunion counselling for our child and our family can help us work through this. Even when everyone is well disposed toward each other, wants only the best for the adoptee, and works hard to cooperate, it is still emotional. And then, it doesn't always go well; we need to prepare for that.

Many of us feel that by contacting the birth mother, we may be tipping a well-balanced cart, and we don't look forward to the resulting chaos. Our child has always seemed so stable and happy, and surely bringing the birth family into her life is going to "upset" everything. Yes, it is. But if she can't bring the birth family into her life, she is going to be upset in any case. The need to belong, the need to know her birth family, and the need to find her origins is only going to disturb her emotionally more and more as she matures. Adoptees tell us reunion is necessary. Intellectually, most of us can accept this and agree it is necessary. Not all, of course. I have met adoptive parents who still believe that anything that happened before their child arrived in their family was irrelevant and any reactions from their child are unwarranted. But most of us recognize that our child needs to connect, so we try to facilitate a meeting.

That doesn't make it comfortable. We can long for the days

when all we had to do was cuddle and comfort and all was well. As our child moves into the teen years and early adulthood, comfort becomes more complicated.

Some parents may fear their child will abandon them and transfer their love and affections to their first parents. Statistics show this seldom happens, and my own research with teens showed they were not looking for a new set of parents when they searched. But feelings are not rational, and adoptive parents may actively fear this.

Adoptive parents may also fear they haven't enough emotional strength to deal with the onslaught of feelings that will come their way. The author Kerry Greenwood said it well in a novel: "My skin tries to crawl off me and find a more compassionate human."[1] We wish someone else would take on the responsibility, take on the upheaval that comes with reunion, but we must face this part of our child's life, and trust, if the reunion is disastrous, it will at least give our child some peace, a sense of belonging, and identity. And, if all goes well, he will stay close and easy with us.

Some part of us recognizes the birth parents have a vested interest in our child. We are mutually parents, albeit with different responsibilities and emotional attachments. Our possessive she-bear or he-bear attitudes serve our children well when they are young, but we must relax those attitudes when they get older. We need to hold on to our fierce and loyal attachment while letting go of our possessive stance. Our children are people, not property. What will make them happy and contented with their position in society? We may almost choke on conflicting emotions, caught amidst what we know is good for our child, our fear they will be hurt by rejection, and our own fears that the birth family will be more loving, more attractive, and preferred. We need courage and support. It's difficult.

For adoptive parents, a little self-reflection is imperative. What are we prepared to do to assist our child in this reunion? How much contact would make us comfortable? We may well push ourselves beyond our comfort point in order to satisfy our child, but it helps to recognize feelings and set boundaries before going into the reunion so we aren't blindsided by overwhelming emotions.

We can rely on our usual successful methods of handling emotions: a day at the spa, a long walk, playing music, a hard afternoon on the basketball court, talk, talk, talk with our best friend—whatever works. We should just schedule time for it; we'll need it.

We need to make sure our child's adoptive family, including our extended family, is aware of the search and the pending reunion. We must put out fires in the extended family before our child knows about them. The goal is to have everyone stay calm and supportive.

Use Your Support Network

We need the support of others who understand the reunion process. Those in our adoptive parent support group can validate our feelings and give suggestions on how to make the process go more smoothly. They also may allow us to vent our own suppressed frustrations, a normal part of parenting, which can be compressed into unmanageable pressure by the stress of a reunion.

The birth mother's readiness

It may be a challenge to ask our child, especially if he or she is a teen, to consider the birth mother's point of view. Some teens are truly compassionate, but others are notoriously the centre of their universe and have not yet developed the mental agility to put themselves in another's place. Have the talk about the birth mother's feelings well in advance. She suffered too and may still be suffering. We can talk about the information we do have on his birth family and point out that it is outdated. Also, what the social workers thought were his birth mother's motivations in placing him for adoption may not have been accurate, and she may be grieving her loss.

If the child cannot appreciate what the birth mother may have felt or might feel at the reunion, we can put forward some rational points he might appreciate. His birth mother may be unable to respond well to a reunion because his birth represented pain, abandonment by her family, and great loneliness. Meeting him would bring these feelings back, and she may not want to experience them again. Keeping him at a distance may be her way of protecting herself. A birth mother is not just a repository of information—even if your child may view her that way. Advise him to be considerate.

It would be wise to discuss the following with your child. Now bear in mind, my boys would not discuss anything with me, but I started on this too late for them to be comfortable. I assume you have started talking about this while your child is still early in their teens. Here is what I wish I had discussed with mine:

Think about how you want to include your birth mother and your birth family in your life. Do you want her to come to family gatherings? How much contact do you want? What kind of relationship would make you feel comfortable? What do you think she and your birth family will want?

People are not perfect. The birth mother and her family aren't perfect, and neither are we. We have to work out the reunion the best way we can, which means planning, talking, being considerate, and seeing it as part of a long-term process.

The Search for Origins

Most parents accept that our children need to find their beginnings, and we can help them. It is easier for them if we are listening, offering options, and supporting their quest.

Searching for original name

This process is not equal or fair across North America. Some provinces in Canada have open records: British Columbia, Alberta, Yukon Territories, Ontario, and Newfoundland.[2] No consent by anyone is necessary for adult adoptees looking to find their original name. The ability to get the original birth certificate with the original name varies in other provinces. It may be moot in the Northwest Territories and Nunavut—social workers there tell me that everyone knows everyone anyway. In jurisdictions where it is possible, an adoptee the age of nineteen or older can apply for his or her birth certificate, which will have the original name on it. An adult adoptee can get that piece of paper in about six weeks in British Columbia, as long as a disclosure veto is not on file. A birth mother can file such a veto and so prevent an adoptee from finding her, although this is rare.[3, 4] Fees for certificates will vary by province; as of this writing, it is $50 in BC.

In the US, several states—Alaska, Kansas, Maine, Tennessee, Alabama, Delaware, New Hampshire, and Oregon—also have this original certificate service. There may be others, as attitudes and laws change. Check with the Child Gateway Information website.[5] They have an easy-to-use state-by-state process for finding information. In some states, it is difficult to get information without a court order; in other states, it is a matter of sending in a request. For example, Kansas law states:

Access to Original Birth Certificate.
Citation: Ann. Stat. § 65-2423
The original birth certificate is a sealed document that may be
opened by the State Registrar only upon the demand of the adult
adopted person or by an order of the court.[6]

Which, translated into everyday language, means: just ask for it. It's amazing that different jurisdictions can vary so greatly in their support of adoptees and birth families. The success or failure for getting this kind of information really depends on where you live.

Social media

Social media is invaluable, but you need to be very clear about what you want to know. "Male adoptee, born June 25, 1970, St. Paul's Hospital, Vancouver BC, searching for birth family" is specific and tells Google what is important. You can blog this information yourself, use it in your correspondence, and place it on various sites. You can contact one or several of the many adoption search and reunion sites and register with them. Most of the search sites will help you at no cost. There are rafts of them. One site lists ways in which you can search public records.[7]

Be sure to register your child on the International Soundex Reunion Registry,[8] which is free. There are also many other sites where adoptees and birth parents can register. Put your child's name or suggest your child put his or her name on as many sites as you can find, particularly if they are free. I'm emphasizing "free" as there are a lot of sites that offer to search for a fee. Some don't guarantee a result, which means you can throw your money away, and some ask for payment only upon success. Know what you can do for yourself without charge before you commit money to these companies. When you pay a fee, you may feel you have transferred the responsibility of searching to a company, but that doesn't mean they will do the search or that they will do it any more successfully than you could.

"Search angels" are volunteers who donate their time and resources to helping adoptees search for their family members; they are often knowledgeable, competent, and helpful, and will assist you at no cost.[9] It's amazing how much help is available.

Use the information you have. Even if it is sometimes wrong, it is what you have so start with it. Search records online. This, believe me, is tedious. I tried several sites and found myself spending hours scrolling through names and dates. It is sometimes captivating, as I imagine stories behind some of the names and get distracted from my focus of finding "Baby boy, born June 27, 1967" and start to wonder what happened to "Baby girl, born Jun 26, 1967." This is the burden of the imaginative; we get sidetracked by our own fantasies. Asking for help from a search angel might be a good place to start. Getting on adoption search sites with others who are doing the same thing will help you persist.

Start your own blog

For the computer competent, create a domain and begin a blog that enlists as many as possible to search with you. Link it to your Facebook page, or create a new page and feed all Twitter and other media through your blog. Engage with other searchers and, behold, you have created a team. Claudia Corrigan D'Arcy (*Musings of the Lame*) gives excellent advice on how to do this.[10]

Contacting the birth mother and/or family

Without an original birth certificate, we have to find the birth mother. If we do have a name, it may take some time to find the person attached to that name. Unless our child was dropped off at the door in a basket or found in the bulrushes, we have the name of the hospital where he was born, his birth date, time, and weight, the name of the adoption agency, and some information about his birth parents. Details can be important. If our child's birth mother was the youngest of seven siblings, that may help. If his father was a tugboat captain, that bit of information might point us in the right direction.

My eldest son's family history contained a note that his birth father's brother won the provincial junior wrestling championship and he was blind. I thought there must be only one person in the province who fit that description. I still can't find him, but I'm looking. I found a man who had been a blind wrestler in the correct year and contacted his brother. Wonderful man, but not the right one. Sometimes small pieces of information are very helpful and sometimes they are not. It is a time-consuming process and can be discouraging as we run into uncooperative people, closed files, misleading information, and downright lies.

Finding medical information

When you need medical information from your child's birth family, you may find your search easier. Many states allow an adoptee or adoptive parents to search for the birth parents when the purpose of the search is to find medical information. Some states require you start a court action to open up the records, but the courts will grant the order based on the imperative nature of your request. In the provinces where adoption information is not readily available, some provisions are made to apply to the Ministry under "severe medical conditions" for release of information. This is not consistent throughout the country. In other jurisdictions, you simply search your hospital records.

You can't lie about it—that would be perjury—you must really need that information. Times are changing, so you might inquire if your state or province is more amenable to a request now than in the past and if a court order is still necessary.

First Nations status or enrolment in a US Native tribe

In Canada, if you know or suspect your child is of First Nations descent, he can obtain his status number from the Department of Indigenous and Northern Affairs. From this source you can determine his band membership, and the band can tell you his family name and his mother's name.

This is how we found my youngest son's birth mother. He applied for his status number. That gave him the name and location of his tribe. I approached a band council worker who took my letter to his birth mother and asked for contact. His birth mother had not told other members of the band about him, so she needed time to prepare the people around her but was willing to meet him. And, the band worker told me, she indicated she'd be thrilled to meet him. Her family held a meeting. The worker told me his mother talked and listened to others, all the time petting the picture I had sent. The uncles and aunts began to make contact and came to dinner. My son went north to meet his birth mother and more aunts and cousins and his sister. He found a place waiting for him as a member of the family. His uncle took him out on the family territories and showed him the traditional lands. They could not have been kinder. This all took place about ten years after it should have, as I hadn't realized earlier how important it was.

Métis children who have Aboriginal ancestry but are not First Nations or Inuit may be registered with the Métis Council of Canada. The Inuit do not have a registry. In the US, the Bureau of Indian Affairs does not keep a central registry for American

Indians or Alaskan Natives. When you search, you must know which tribe your child may be enrolled in. When she was adopted, the adoption agency or lawyer involved in the placement was supposed to inform the tribal council, so the child should appear in the tribal records. This isn't simple, but there are volunteers online who will help. If your child contacts the lawyer or the agency that made the placement, they will likely give her the information.

The Reunion

A reunion typically involves a birth mother, adoptee, and adoptive parents who have had no contact throughout the adoptee's life. This is a meeting of those who have held each other in their imaginations for years. The mental vision and the reality might be very different, so all need to be prepared for this.

I had no idea who I was going to meet. When I first met my youngest son's birth family, I felt nervous and a little shaky, not sure of what the family expected from me. I know my son felt the same, and only time ironed out that anxiety. That first meeting seemed a bit overwhelming. I spoke with a counsellor in his birth mother's Native community and got a lot of support from her. She told me about the family and what my son could expect from them. They are emotionally generous people so I knew they would not deliberately hurt him. I suppose that is the first thing adoptive parents want to know: Will my child be safe?

Our first meeting was with his uncles, an aunt, and a cousin. It was a polite encounter, and my son was at great pains to let them know he was already part of our family and not willing to change allegiance. They appreciated that, but his uncle took me aside and let some of his anger at white people adopting Natives spill onto me. I responded by saying I wasn't holding the whole race on my back and that I wanted to have a reasonable relationship with him.

I truly liked my son's uncle; I prefer a straight accusation rather than hidden resentment, and he came straight at me. He agreed we wouldn't solve the greater issue of race relations within our family, and my son came to know and like his birth family.

Other than the fact that my son's birth mother was four-foot-eleven and Native, I had no vision of her. I should have known that my handsome son had a beautiful mother, but I hadn't thought about it. She was not only beautiful, she was also kind, loving, generous, and straightforward. After we met we sat in the local pub and talked. My son introduced us to the group there as "my mothers. She had me; she raised me," pointing to us in turn. He wandered off at one point, and I asked his mother, "Why didn't you try to find him?"

She answered, "I promised not to."

That was heartbreaking. I had no idea such a promise would have prevented her from looking for us. I know now other birth mothers feel, or have been made to feel, they don't have the right to look for contact. We might have met years ago if each of us had felt we had a right to connect. We talked a lot that night. While we don't stay in touch now, we did for years, and I hold her in my heart.

What is a successful reunion?

It may be one that satisfies your child, allows her to grow and mature, and contributes to her acceptance of herself as a member of her family, her society, and her country. Insofar as a reunion with her birth family supports those goals, it is successful for the adoptee.

If it brings satisfaction to the birth mother, allows her to mitigate some of the pain and loss she felt at the child's birth, and contributes to her feelings of being accepted as a mother, then it is successful for her.

If adoptive parents remain close to their child and secure in their position as parents, and feel supported by the birth mother and birth family in loving concern for their child, then it is successful for them.

How does your child want the meeting to occur?

Does he or she want you there for the first meeting? Waiting in the car? Not around at all? Talk about it well beforehand.

My son's first meeting with his birth mother took place when he contacted his birth sister and said he'd like to go to her northern community and meet his birth mother. She agreed that it would be a good idea and would let her mom know. His adopted sister said she would drive him the eighteen hours to their remote community, so they piled into the car and took off.

This meeting came about suddenly. My son just decided one weekend he wanted to meet her. There had been preparatory work. He had met his uncles and an aunt and cousin. I had talked with the counsellor in the community who was a friend of his birth mother. He didn't arrive out of the blue. She knew he was coming. When they arrived, my son was driving. He didn't know the way to his birth sister's house, so they had to ask directions. They didn't have any pictures of his birth mother, but they knew she was short, and a short Native woman was waiting at the side of the road, the mountains towering over her, no one else for miles. My daughter said she had a tingling sensation. My son had no premonition and simply pulled over to ask for directions.

"Can you tell me, please, where Susan Jones[11] [his sister] lives?"

The woman looked directly at him and said, "Are you D—?"

He got out of the car and stood beside her. "Are you L—?"

She nodded. My son leaned his six-foot-one body down and hugged this tiny four-foot-eleven-inch woman. My daughter sat in the car and watched them. She said *she* was crying; she didn't know about the other two.

Often we are advised to be emotionally light and a little distant at the initial visit. Easy to say; it's like saying "stay calm" when the tornado is heading straight at you. It will help if you know how to calm yourself, how to speak reasonably, and how to ease into a relationship, but, no question, this meeting does matter, and its very importance can create apprehension.

Adoptive parents who are supporting children in their search and the adoptees themselves must understand this meeting of birth mother and adoptee is fraught with emotions for the birth mother as well as the adoptee. She will have her own way of handling emotions, and they may not be advantageous to our child. Because reunions are steeped in a boiling potage of sensations, expect rage, fear, disappointment, joy, love, shock, rejection, and appreciation—even all at once. It is normal to feel a great deal. Talk to others who have gone through the process, and be prepared. No, you are not crazy; you are reacting to strong stimuli. And so is your child's birth mother. After the initial meeting, proceed slowly. Your child and his birth mother need to process their reactions, and that takes time.

Getting specific information

Find others whose family constellation looks like yours. If your child was born to a black family and then adopted into your white family, find others who have a similar history. How did they handle their reunions? What specific concerns did they have? Can you talk to this group about your concerns? Can your child talk to this group? Perhaps she should attend sessions without you. What do they advise?

Contact the adoption agency that placed your child many

years ago and ask them for counselling. Your local adoptive families association may have a support group that can help. My local group has peer support for parents and specific online groups for transracial families. They also have an adoption coordinator who can direct us to the support we need. I was looking for an out-of-province support group for my son and she found an address for me. This service has grown mightily in the last decade.

Adoptive parents need to ask for help. Rarely does someone come to us to offer it. But long gone are the days when no agency was interested in you after the adoption was finalized. Today's adoptive parents can benefit from joining adoptive parents' groups, even if only online. It helps to get specific information.

Getting counselling

Adoptive parents can benefit from counselling sessions with their child, and sometimes without their child. Pick a counsellor who is knowledgeable about adoption. If you can't find anyone—you may live in a rural community where there is no one—find someone who listens well and talk about your concerns. Online and Skype communication helps, but you still need to find a counsellor who listens and can advise you.

Making a plan for the future

If an adopted child is willing to have a new relative in his life, how much contact does he or she want? What does the birth mother want? When I talked to birth mothers, they all seemed to want as much contact as they could get, but those who volunteered to talk to me were those who were looking for a relationship. Those who don't want contact obviously wouldn't volunteer to talk to me, so I have gleaned their opinions from online forums where it is clear some birth mothers refuse contact. This is inconceivable to adoptive parents who can't see why anyone wouldn't want contact with their wonderful child, but it happens.

Some adoptees don't want much contact with their birth mother. They want to know who she is, but don't want a relationship, or much of one. It may be that adoptive parents can respect this wish of their child while at the same time keeping contact with the birth mother, keeping her informed of their child's life and activities, without facilitating meetings. It would need agreement from the child. That way, the birth mother or birth family can have a loose affiliation without transgressing the boundaries set by the child. There are many possibilities in this family constellation. Mutual respect is vital here. And if the adopted child is in the teen years or young adulthood, the relationship is unlikely to be under the parents' control. The child will direct and manage it.

What Does Love Have to Do with It?

While love is not enough to give an adopted child security and a sense of identity, it goes a long way toward making this complicated family constellation useful and supportive. Love must marry truth for a family to be comfortable with their relatives. Secrecy makes trouble. A reunion brings the secrets into the open and shrinks their influence.

Honesty and love are the propelling powers in a reunion. The Native people of my son's nation conclude meetings with an intonation spoken by the leader and answered by the group.

The leader says, "All my relations."

The group responds, "All my relations."

I interpret that to mean each person is bringing to this gathering their ancestors and living relatives as a cohesive power. It *feels* powerful when I raise my hands and say, "All my relations." I think of my children, their partners, their children, my sixty cousins, and my aunts and uncles in my huge extended family, as I invoke the power of family to come to me at this place. Our children need all their relatives. I know it's intangible, not measurable. It's a feeling. Still, I believe I am united with everyone at the meeting in that feeling, and all their relatives. Perhaps that's love.

1   Kerry Greenwood, *Earthly Delights* (Scottsdale, AZ: Poisoned Pen Press, 1992), p. 6.

2   "Searching and Reuniting." Adoption Council of Canada. [No date.] http://adoption.ca/searching-and-reuniting

3   "Information for Adults Adopted in British Columbia." Ministry of Children and Family Development, British Columbia. [No date.] http://mcf.gov.bc.ca/adoption/info_adults.htm

4   "Adoption Records." Vital Statistics Agency, British Columbia. [No date.] http://www2.gov.bc.ca/gov/topic.page?id=8B3879BB27074769AE0842D9ACE-CF6D9

5   "Access to Adoption Records." Washington, DC: US Department of Health and Human Services, Children's Bureau, Child Welfare Information Gateway. [No date.] http://childwelfare.gov/topics/systemwide/laws-policies/state

6   Ibid.

7   Priscilla Stone Sharp, "Finding Living Relatives and Adoption-Related Searches Using Public Records on the Internet." March 6, 2014. http://priscillasharp.blogspot.ca/

8   International Soundex Reunion Registry. http://www.isrr.org

9   Sharp, "Finding Living Relatives ..."

10 Claudia Corrigan Darcy, "How to Use Social Media for an Adoption Search," *Musings of the Lame*, March 13, 2014. http://adoptionbirthmothers.com/how-to-use-social-media-for-an-adoption-search/

11 Not her real name.

9 The Future of Adoption

Adoption appears to be accepted in most countries of the world with the exception of Muslim countries where children are placed with relatives, in the care of friends, in institutions, or abandoned.[1] In those countries there is a provision for guardianship so that a family can care for a child, but they cannot give him or her the family name, and the child cannot inherit as if a child of the family. This makes adopting from those countries close to impossible. Of the remaining countries, ninety-four promote standards that follow the Hague Convention.[2] They have protocols that protect children and curb those who would profit from buying and selling children, from coercing pregnant women, or from pressuring poverty-stricken families to sell a child. Many governments are trying to put regulations in place so adoptive parents and adoptees can be assured that the birth parents willingly agreed to the adoption. The regulations aren't yet universally reliable. Angelina Jolie's child Zahara was given up for adoption by her grandmother without, it was discovered later, her mother's consent. When her birth mother was finally located, she did consent to the adoption.[3] It could have been messy and heartbreaking for all those involved.

It will take time to make changes, but awareness of problems is a mighty impetus to change, and we are now more aware than ever of the need to prevent the exploitation of children and adoptive parents.

The Changing Philosophy

Adoptive parents may be shocked to hear that there is a backlash against adoption. Bloggers tell us that not only should we not adopt racially different children, we should not adopt *any* child because we are ripping the child away from the mother. Forums on the Internet and opinion pieces in magazines and newspapers demand to know why "pulling children away from their birth families" is allowed. They point out that many organizations are profiting by such transactions. Adoptive parents are generally depicted as white, rich, uncaring, and the only ones who benefit.

How could the picture of adoptive parents get so twisted? Probably because there is a grain of truth in it—but only a grain. Adoption does benefit the adoptive parents almost always. It benefits birth parents as well, but perhaps not every time, as there are some instances in which both the child and the birth family would be better off to keep the child in the original home. Adoptees benefit much of the time, but not, I suspect, every time. It still seems outlandish to condemn the adoption process, which helps so many, because it does not help a few. Birth mothers are portrayed in this scathing condemnation as vulnerable and without power. That may be true of some, but not all. This is an oversimplification of a complex world. We need to pay attention to Adam Pertman's view that every family should have the support they need to be successful. If we concentrate on that philosophy we could strive to provide the best family for every child, including families of origin, adoptive families, and foster families.

I do know that when I adopted my sons, their mothers suffered. I didn't cause that suffering, but yes, I was complicit in it. If society had offered more support to those mothers, perhaps they would not have relinquished their boys. Perhaps. But both had family pressure to place their babies for adoption; their families could not support them. They were young—one seventeen, one eighteen. They couldn't support themselves, and adoption seemed a good choice. In hindsight, I can see that more financial assistance and a more accepting social attitude might have prevented the placements, but there wasn't much support or acceptance, so adoption was the best choice at the time. We adoptive parents didn't know the effect adoption would have on our children or their birth mothers, and we certainly did not believe we were part of a sinister plot against children. We were doing what seemed reasonable and loving at the time. We were happy; the baby was happy. We didn't know what the placement agency had told the birth mothers. We did not knowingly cause her harm.

Open adoption has mitigated many of the problems the old secret placements created. Birth families can now support the child in ways they can manage, and the babies can still have a secure and legal place in the adopted family. I can't see the objection to open adoption. I still get an itchy feeling between my shoulder blades when I am around people who blame adoptive parents for baby trafficking. It's reassuring to remember most of the fifty teenagers I interviewed said that they loved their adoptive parents and were glad they landed in that particular family.

We need to mitigate the effects of separation on the birth mother and on the adoptee. We know they may have difficulties with this. Biological children aren't perfect either. Our local gangster bosses are a family of biological brothers who come from a middle-class home. In fact, I suspect most of the gangsters, of which there are many in my area, are biological children. Many of the wayward members of society are biological children. Biological children are not problem-free.[4]

It may be that the backlash against adoption will gain ground, and adoption will be seen as exploitive. If so, many children will be abandoned or neglected. Both the US and Canada are drifting away from the dream of an egalitarian society where all have enough to live on and social supports and Medicare are available to everyone. We are widening the rift between the wealthy and the poor and diminishing the middle class. If a social prejudice against adoption develops along with an increasingly impoverished society and a rise in the cost of adoption, fewer children will find homes, and the social costs will be enormous.

We need to advocate for more open and transparent adoptions and for more community involvement in welcoming adopted children. We need to talk about it with as many as we can so that adoption is simply another way to have a family—and definitely not a secret. If it is part of an open society and accepted in that society, the backlash will drop away.

Profiting from Adoption

The adoption process has attracted some profiteers. Today, adoptions cost a packet of money, and that money attracts business. In Canada, the cost can be only the registration fees—up to $3,000 for a public agency and foster care adoption, or between $10,000 and $20,000 for a licenced private-agency domestic adoption. It is not legal for an adoptive parent to pay a birth mother in Canada[5] so the costs are for the adoption process only. International adoptions processed by private agencies can run between $20,000 and $30,000 plus the cost of getting to the child's country and staying there for some time.

In the US, costs can run from nothing to $2,500 for public agency and foster care adoptions, between $5,000 and $40,000 or more for a licenced private agency domestic adoption, or $8,000 to $40,000 or more for an independent adoption such as a lawyer-directed adoption. A facilitated/unlicenced adoption, which is an adoption arranged by someone without a licence and no supervisory agency to govern them, can cost between $5,000 and $40,000, but these are illegal in some states. International adoptions can cost between $15,000 and $30,000.[6]

Some adoptive parents have additional costs paid to the birth mother (legal in the US). They can pay for the medical care of several women's pregnancies before one birth mother places her baby with them. Adoption can be hugely expensive. Often, adoptive parents have just come through the expenses of IVF treatments and have to go for that second mortgage to pay for adoption expenses.

It seems adoption as a business has erupted as the number of newborn babies available for adoption has plummeted. This has created a "business" opportunity for many entrepreneurs. Sometimes I'm embarrassed to be related even by species to people who coerce the vulnerable to give up their babies, change and obliterate records, create total fantasy bios for the children, and then profit from it.

Luckily, there are hardworking, competent adoption workers who sincerely try to act in the best interests of the children. The difficulty for us as adoptive parents is that we are so anxious to work through the system to find our child, we tend to overlook or ignore problems that don't seem quite right in order to get to that child. A little research on the agency before any money changes hands is prudent. It's hard to do that after we are already engaged with the agency, when our names are on a waiting list, and we are getting encouraging pictures of babies. It's easy to ignore any warning signs that the agency may not be honest or reliable. There is a website for US adoption agencies that rates and reviews them. The site is worth checking out. I was encouraged by the honesty of one review that said: "Our experience with the domestic side of [the agency] could not have been more frustrating, unprofessional, inconsiderate, and borders on fraud. Twice we were given referrals for birth mothers who we were told were 'squeaky clean, no red flags' and both times turned out to be drug addicts, liars, and the second one was simultaneously taking money from another couple through another agency."[7]

Now that's a review! There are no doubt others, but I could find no corresponding rating system for Canadian adoption agencies.

The Matching Game

The profiles aren't the person. The descriptions of adoptable children you read online aren't the person you see, smell, trade unspoken communications with, or bond with. Anyone who has had experience with online dating will agree that what you see in the profile online is rarely who you find at the coffee date. The online parade of pictures of adoptable children smacks of the same market mentality. I haven't reasoned it out very well, but my skin reacts when I look at the photos of all these children who are "lovely," "sweet," and "looking for love." I'm told the parade of pictures is highly effective in finding good homes and that agencies protect the children by having the pictures embedded with watermarks and codes so they don't disappear into the "dark web" where they can be exploited or where the child, particularly an older child, can be tracked.[8]

I am less bothered by and, in fact, encouraged by the profiles potential parents put online for a birth mother to peruse. She will be making the choice, and some information, and sometimes a lot of information, can help her make that choice. Potential adoptive parents don't know what aspect of their lives will appeal to the birth mother, so they might as well portray their lives honestly.

There is always the chance that a birth mother who is not registered with an agency might pull up the website and pick them from the list. It is still wise to go through a licenced agency so that everyone's rights are protected and expectations are clear and legal.

The Internet is going to be part of adoption placement, contact with adoptive and birth families, support, and search and reunion in more and more useful ways. I trust we will be able to smack down the predators, keep the children and families safe, and secure legal protection for all. Exposure by bloggers such as Claudia Corrigan D'Arcy will help to keep honest people honest and warn against the unscrupulous. There is potential for harm on the Internet, but perhaps more potential for good as secrets are much harder to keep today than in the past, and secrets were what caused so much harm.

Family Coherence

Adoptive parents seldom look for a match, such as blond hair and blue eyes, with their family. When the birth was a secret, matching was important so no one could tell your child was adopted. Today we are less interested in having the perfectly matched family. Many of our biological families are mixed with step-children and half-siblings so that many families no longer look alike. Even biologically related families don't necessarily look alike. A woman of my acquaintance who is black said that one of her three biological children has very light skin. She was asked more than once, "Where'd you get that white baby?" Variations in biological families are common. More biological families are transracial, and interracial marriages are common today—more in some areas of North America than others, but still not unusual. I expect they will be much more common in the future. Transracial adopted children may still be obvious in some families, but they won't be as remarkable as they were.

Adoptive families have challenges common to biological families in raising children. It costs much more than we expect to raise them and get them off to college or on to their first job. We all have problems; no one gets dealt the perfect hand. We struggle with a school system that is absolutely wrong for our child. We suffer in the emergency room while we wait for a diagnosis. We cry over their first broken love affair; we agonize over their life choices; we freak out after a call from the police. (It does happen. You swear your kid won't do anything stupid, but then they do.) We muddle through all that with the joys of parenthood to sustain us. We raise compassionate, thoughtful, wise children, and wonder how that happened.

Adoptive parents have the same problem of divorce that biological parents have, and they too have to try to keep their families functioning after divorce. If the father leaves the family, he may still visit and give support to the children—and he may not. This can be a shock to adoptees who have already lost a birth mother; the loss of another parent can be catastrophic. If the family has had an open adoption, the birth parents can be very helpful during this time, reassuring the adoptee that he has not been abandoned by everyone. Those of us securely bonded with our adopted children find it hard to believe that adoptive parents can leave their children, but they do. Some people believe they can wander off and reinvent themselves as a different person without the baggage of a former family. This is when the extended family, including the birth family, can help to support the children. Reliable, loving relatives are truly valuable. Divorce is common. Perhaps, as adoptive parents, we need to make contingent plans for our children if one parent leaves. We may want to reach out to birth parents and extended birth family relatives. They have no legal rights, but they may have strong emotional attachments and feelings of responsibility that could help the children. This might be rare, but it might be possible in some situations.

Love and Quantum Physics

It seems to me that love is messy, mixed up, blossoming, and receding, never still and calm. If we hold in mind that our children are encompassed in our love, buoyed by it, and we similarly are encompassed in their love and buoyed by it, we can appreciate its strength. Holding a vision of our child as healthy, whole, content, and happy will help us react to our child in ways that allow them to develop that way. I am not negating the many choices, challenges, crazy ideas, and weird options that come across our path in parenting, but I believe it is our fierce love that helps our child find a strong emotional centre and leads him or her to a secure place in the world.

The notion that we can actualize energy with intention (a tenet of quantum physics, meditation, and prayer) seems to describe love. If we look for it in our children, we will find it. Perhaps we need a science that can describe love more clearly than as a sentimental idea or an elusive concept. I believe it is a robust and creative drive. I hope that we may find rigorous evidence of the strength and necessity of love to justify our intuitive understanding of how love supports and sustains our families.

We have a vision of our family and our children. We have expectations, and we work at realizing them. How our children view themselves is the reality they will create. The vision we have for our family is the one we create. We knew it all along. We can make a loving family.

1   Muzammil H. Siddiqi, "Adopting under Islamic Faith," *International Adoption Guide*. [No date.] http://www.internationaladoptionguide.co.uk/from-which-countries-is-it-possible-to-adopt-from/islamic-adoption.html

2   "Convention Countries." Intercountry Adoption. Bureau of Consular Affairs. US Department of State. [No date.] http://travel.state.gov/content/adoptionsabroad/en/hague-convention/convention-countries.html

3   Jacey Fortin, "Adopting from Africa: The Complicated Truth Behind a Celebrity Fad," *International Business Times*, May 30, 2012. http://www.ibtimes.com/adopting-africa-complicated-truth-behind-celebrity-fad-705521

4   Keiron McConnell, personal communication with author, based on his graduate studies research with gangs.

5   "FAQ." Adoption Council of Canada. [No date.] http://adoption.ca/faqs

6   "Costs of Adopting." Washington, DC: Child Welfare Information Gateway. [No date.] http://childwelfare.gov/pubpdfs/s_costs.pdf

7   "Adoption Agency Ratings." [No date.] http://adoptionagencyratings.com/top-rated-listings

8   Beverly Gmerek and Kristin Griffin Jones, personal communications at North American Council of Adoption Children's Conference, August 1, 2015.

Further Reading

Appignanesi, Lisa. *All About Love: Anatomy of an Unruly Emotion.* New York: W.W. Norton & Company, 2011.

Balcom, Karen. *The Traffic in Babies: Cross-border Adoption and Baby-selling between the United States and Canada, 1930–1972.* Toronto: University of Toronto Press, 2011.

Brennan, Deborah A. *Labours of Love: Canadians Talk about Adoption.* Toronto: Dundurn Press, 2008.

Brodzinsky, David M., and Adam Pertman, eds. *Adoption by Lesbians and Gay Men: A New Dimension in Family Diversity.* Oxford, UK: Oxford University Press, 2012.

Brodzinsky, David M., and Jesús Palacios. *Psychological Issues in Adoption: Research and Practice.* (Advances in Applied Developmental Psychology.) Santa Barbara, CA: Praeger, 2005.

Crook, Marion. *The Face in the Mirror: Teens and Adoption.* Vancouver: Arsenal Pulp Press, 2000.

Dennis, Laura, ed. *Adoption Therapy: Perspectives from Clients and Clinicians on Processing and Healing Post-Adoption Issues.* Redondo Beach, CA: Entourage Publishing, 2014.

Fournier, Suzanne, and Ernie Crey. *Stolen from Our Embrace: The Abduction of First Nations Children and the Restoration of Aboriginal Communities.* Vancouver: Douglas & McIntyre, 1998.

Giroux, Henry A. *Disposable Youth, Racialized Memories, and the Culture of Cruelty.* (Framing 21st Century Social Issues.) New York: Routledge, 2012.

Grand, Michael Phillip. *The Adoption Constellations: New Ways of Thinking About and Practicing Adoption.* North Charleston, SC: Createspace, 2011.

Hall, Beth, and Gail Steinberg. *Inside Transracial Adoption: Strength-based, Culture-Sensitizing, Parenting Strategies for Inter-Country or Domestic Adoptive Families that Don't "Match."* Philadelphia: Jessica Kingsley Publishers, 2013.

Hamm, Ronald L. *Analog Medicine: A Science of Healing. Adopting the Logic of Quantum Mechanics as a Medical Strategy.* Bloomington, IN: Authorhouse, 2003.

———. *The Philosophic Foundation of Holistic Medicine: The Deductions.* [n.l.]: R.L. Hamm, 2010.

Kelly, Edward F., Emily Williams Kelly, Adam Crabtree, Alan Gauld, Michael Grosso, and Bruce Greyson. *Irreducible Mind: Toward a Psychology for the 21st Century.* New York: Rowman & Littlefield, 2007.

Kerby, Anthony Paul. *Narrative and the Self.* Bloomington, IN: Indiana University Press, 1991.

Kirk, David H. *Adoptive Kinship: A Modern Institution in Need of Reform.* Port Angeles, WA: Ben-Simon, 1985.

———. *Exploring Adoptive Family Life: The Collected Adoption Papers of H. David Kirk.* Port Angeles, WA: Ben-Simon, 1988.

———. *Shared Fate: A Theory and Method of Adoptive Relationships.* Port Angeles, WA: Ben-Simon, 1964, 1984.

Lewis, Marc. *Biology of Desire: Why Addiction Is Not a Disease.* Toronto: Doubleday Canada, 2015.

Myss, Caroline. *Anatomy of the Spirit: The Seven Stages of Power and Healing.* New York: Three Rivers Press, 1996.

Melina, Lois Ruskai. *Making Sense of Adoption: A Parent's Guide.* New York: Harper & Row, 1989.

———. *The Open Adoption Experience.* New York: Perennial Library, 1993.

Nuttgens, Simon. "Stories of Aboriginal Transracial Adoption." *The Qualitative Report,* 18 (2013): 1–17.

Pertman, Adam. *Adoption Nation: How the Adoption Revolution is Transforming Our Families—and America.* Boston: The Harvard Common Press, 2011.

Purvis, Karyn B., Davie R. Cross, and Wendy Lyons Sunshine. *The Connected Child: Bring Hope and Healing to Your Adoptive Family.* New York: McGraw Hill, 2007.

Purvis, Laura, ed. *Adoption Therapy: Perspectives from Clients and Clinicians Processing and Healing Post-Adoption Issues.* Redondo Beach, CA: Entourage Publishing, Inc., 2014.

Putman, Robert D. *Bowling Alone: The Collapse and Revival of American Community.* New York: Simon & Schuster, 2000.

Siegel, Daniel J., and Mary Hartzell. *Parenting from the Inside Out: How a Deeper Self-understanding Can Help You Raise Children Who Thrive.* New York: J. P. Tarcher/Penguin, 2003.

Soll, Joe. *Adoption Healing: A Path to Recovery, Supplement.* College Station, TX: Virtualbookworm.com, 2012.

Swidrovich, Cheryl Marlene. "Positive Experiences of First Nations Children in Non-Aboriginal Foster or Adoptive Care: De-Constructing the 'Sixties Scoop.'" MA dissertation, University of Saskatchewan, 2004.

Tipper, Jenni. "Intentional Fatherhood: Lessons from Gay, Bi, Trans and Queer Dads." *Transition* 42 (Summer 2012): 11.

Verrier, Nancy Newton. *The Primal Wound: Understanding the Adopted Child.* Baltimore, MD: Gateway Press, 1993.

Index

Marion Crook began her career as a public health nurse in Cariboo country, British Columbia. After her Bachelor of Science in Nursing degree, she took a Masters of Liberal Studies and a PhD in Education. She taught nursing, particularly research in nursing, for many years. She is the author of numerous books for adults and teens, both fiction and non-fiction, including two published by Arsenal Pulp Press, *The Face in the Mirror: Teens and Adoption* and *Out of the Darkness: Teens Talk About Suicide*.

marioncrookauthor.com